CHRIST THE BRIDEGROOM
AND THE CHURCH HIS BRIDE

CHRIST THE BRIDEGROOM
AND THE CHURCH HIS BRIDE

A study of the Jewish roots, Biblical texts, and Christian rituals

Prepared by:

BISHOY BOULOS

MTh, Professor of Old Testament

ST SHENOUDA PRESS
SYDNEY, AUSTRALIA
2024

Christ the Bridegroom and The Church His Bride
By: Bishoy Boulos

COPYRIGHT ©2024
St Shenouda Press

All rights reserved. Except for brief quotations in critical publications or reviews, no part of this book may be reproduced in any manner without prior written permission from the publisher.

ST SHENOUDA PRESS
8419 Putty Rd,
Putty, NSW, 2330
Sydney, Australia

www.stshenoudapress.com

ISBN 13: 978-1-7635450-9-0

All scripture quotations, unless otherwise indicated, are taken from the New King James Version. Copyright © 1982 by Thomas Nelson, Inc. Used by permission. All rights reserved.

Table of Contents

Dedication vii

Appreciation viii

Introduction x

Chapter 1: Jehovah Makes a Covenant with Israel 1

The Beginning of the Covenant between the Bride and the Bridegroom 1

Reminding the Prophets of the Relationship of the Bridegroom with His bride 4

Renewing the Covenant 11

Chapter 2: Love in the Song of Songs 15

The Jewish Perspective of the Book 15

The Song's Bridegroom and Bride 18

The Bridegroom in the Jewish Prayers 21

Chapter 3: Christ Betroths the Bride 23

Christ, the Church's Bridegroom 23

Step 1: Choosing the Bride 27

Step 2: Paying the Dowry 32

Step 3: The Covenant and Ketuba 40

Step 4: The Bride's Approval 43

Step 5: The Covenant's Cup 45

Step 6: The Bridegroom's Gifts to the Bride 48

Step 7: The Mikvah 51

Step 8: The Bridegroom's departure 57

Chapter 4: Christ Returns to Take the Bride 61
    The Bride's Waiting Period 61
    The Bridegroom's Return 70
    The Bridal Chamber and the Canopy 75
    The Wedding Banquet 84

Chapter 5: An Inspiration from the Bridegroom and the Bride 87
    The Wedding of Cana 87
    The Last Supper 95
    The Samaritan Woman 98
    The Sufferings and Crucifixion events 110
    The Sadducees' Questions Regarding the Resurrection ...122
    Christian Marriage 127
    Virginity 134
    Christ the Bridegroom in the Song of Songs 138

Chapter 6: The Bridegroom and the Bride in Church Rituals 143
    The Divine Liturgy is a journey beyond time with the Bridegroom 143
    In Matins Prayer and Raising Vesper Incense 146
    In the Midnight Praise 147
    In the Divine Liturgy 150
    In the Crowning Ceremony 158
    In Ecclesiastical Readings 167
    In the prayers and melodies of the church 173
    Yes, you are also a bride! 176

Dedication

This book is dedicated to our spiritual shepherds, whom we have seen as living images of Christ the Bridegroom and witnessed their unfailing love to the church, the bride.

Appreciation

I remind my beloved wife Dina that the theme of this book was the reason for being introduced to each other. I thank her and my beloved children Petro, Perpetua and Parthenia as they gave me quiet time - once in a blue moon - to complete this work (Psalm 128: 3,4)

> "For your Maker (Hebrew לְעַב - bâ'al - baw-al›) is your husband, The Lord of hosts is His name, and your Redeemer is the Holy One of Israel; He is called the God of the whole earth." (Isaiah 54:5)

> "You yourselves bear me witness, that I said, 'I am not the Christ,' but, 'I have been sent before Him.' He who has the bride is the Bridegroom; (from the Greek νυμφίος - numphios) but the friend of the Bridegroom, who stands and hears him, rejoices greatly because of the Bridegroom's voice. Therefore, this joy of mine is fulfilled. He must increase, but I must decrease." (John 3:28-30)

> [This world is the betrothal ... but the wedding will be in the days of the Messiah][1] (Exodus Rabbah)[2]

> [Were it thy wedding-day before thee, wouldest thou not

---

1 Rabbi Dr. H. Freedman & Maurice Simon: Midrash Rabbah /Exodus, The Soncino Press, 1961, P 204.

2 Shimot Rabbah: תומש הבר מִדְרָשׁ מִדְרָשׁ‎ - is a midrash on the Book of Exodus, consisting of two distinct parts compiled in different eras: the first provides verse-by-verse interpretations of the first ten chapters of the Book of Exodus, while the second offers sermons connected to chapters 12-40. It contains early commentaries on the written book of Exodus and oral traditions as well as literary and legal works by Jewish rabbis.

have disregarded all else, and set about the preparation for the feast? And on the eve of consecrating thy soul to the heavenly Bridegroom, wilt thou not cease from carnal things, that thou mayest win spiritual?]3 (Saint Cyril of Jerusalem in his ceremony to the catechumens before their baptism in the Church of the Holy Sepulcher – in the fourth century CE 4).

[In modern English: If it were your wedding day, would you not have disregarded everything else and started preparing for the wedding day ceremony? And on the evening of the day you consecrate your soul to your heavenly Bridegroom, will you not give up the things of the flesh that you may win those of the spirit?].

---

3 St. Cyril of Jerusalem: Procatechesis/ Prologue to the Catechetical Lectures of our Holy Father Cyril/ The Nicene and Post Nicene Fathers / Series2 / Volume 7 - Books for Ages/ AGES Software - Version 2.0, 1997 – Part 6 / P 110-111.

4 Cyril of Jerusalem: (Greek: Κύρυλλος Α´ Ἱεροσολύμων, Kýrillos A Ierosolýmon; Latin: Cyrillus Hierosolymitanus; c. 313[1] – 386 AD) was a theologian of the early Church. About the end of 350 AD. He succeeded Maximus as Bishop of Jerusalem, but was exiled on more than one occasion due to the enmity of Acacius of Caesarea, and the policies of various emperors. St. Cyril left important writings documenting the instruction of catechumens and the order of the Liturgy in his day.

Introduction

A Jew born in Tarsus Cilicia, brought up at the feet of Gamaliel5, zealous for God, a Pharisee and a son of a Pharisee6 but when he believed in Lord Jesus Christ, he saw Him as a Bridegroom in love with His bride! This Jew was the apostle who wrote the most wonderful words describing Christ in place of a suffering Bridegroom out of love for the sake of His bride, the church. For here is St. Paul addressing the husbands and wives in Ephesus saying:

"Wives, submit to your own husbands, as to the Lord. For the husband is head of the wife, as also Christ is head of the church; and He is the Savior of the body. Therefore, just as the church is subject to Christ, so let the wives be to their own husbands in everything. Husbands, love your wives, just as Christ also loved the church and gave Himself for her, that He might sanctify and cleanse her with the washing of water by the word, that He might present her to Himself a glorious church, not having spot or wrinkle or any such thing, but that she should be holy and without blemish ... For this reason, a man shall leave his father and mother and be joined to his

---

5 Gamaliel: Greek Γαμαλιήλ and Hebrew וְקֹוֹה לאילמג זבר Hebrew name which means God's reward, a Jewish Rabbi, a member of the Sanhedrin, and its chief according to what was mentioned in the Talmud. He was a Pharisee. and one of the most famous Jewish teachers in the first century AD. He was the one who taught law to Saul of Tarsus (the Apostle Paul) before his conversion to Christianity (Acts 22:3). He died in the middle of the same century.

6 Pharisee: In Greek Φαρισαῖος, which means separatist. The Pharisees were one of the sects of the Jews that appeared in the second century BC. They considered themselves separated from the people for their holiness. They used to teach and exhort people, but they adhered to the literalism of the law in interpretation and strictness in preserving the customs they received from those who preceded them. Lord Jesus rebuked them because of their hypocrisy, as they were arrogant, proud of their religious knowledge, and despised the common Jews.

wife, and the two shall become one flesh. This is a great mystery, but I speak concerning Christ and the church." (Ephesians 5:22-27, 31-32)

This is a clear metaphor written by our teacher St. Paul, where we see Lord Jesus as a Bridegroom and the church as His bride, and the crucifixion day as a Jewish wedding! A day when the Bridegroom loved His bride and submitted Himself for her. We notice here that St. Paul described that as a great mystery7. Maybe it's hard for us to understand such a thing since we know the crucified one as God, a master and miracle worker but as a Bridegroom, it may sound weird somehow. Especially since we know for certain that the Lord Jesus lived on earth in celibacy as He didn't have a wife, so who is His bride then? Also, how can we describe the painful crucifixion as a scene of a Bridegroom declaring His love to His bride?

The Jewish background definitely helped the apostle Paul to answer these queries. Likewise, if we wish to see the beauty of this metaphor, we need to replace our eyes with 1st century AD Jewish eyes!

Before that, in the beginning of our Lord's ministry, the forerunner and baptizer, St. John the Baptist –he was one of the 1st century AD Jews– pointed out that Lord Jesus Christ is the Bridegroom, saying:

"He who has the bride is the Bridegroom; but the friend of the Bridegroom, who stands and hears him, rejoices greatly because of the Bridegroom's voice. Therefore, this joy of mine is fulfilled." (John 3:29)

Lord Jesus Christ was a Jew as well and the majority of His audience were Jews too. He who is the greatest teacher of all times used

---

[7] Great mystery: It appears in Greek μυστήριον μέγας - Megas mustērion. The word μυστήριον appears in the New Testament 22 times in the singular form (mystery) and 3 times in the plural form(mysteries). An example is what was mentioned in (Colossians 1:26) "The mystery which has been hidden from ages and from generations, but now has been revealed to His saints."

parables and similes taken from daily Jewish life. With His pure mouth, He declared that He is the Bridegroom as it was mentioned in (Mark 2:18-20):

"The disciples of John and of the Pharisees were fasting. Then they came and said to Him, "Why do the disciples of John and of the Pharisees fast, but Your disciples do not fast?" And Jesus said to them, Can the friends of the Bridegroom fast while the Bridegroom is with them? As long as they have the Bridegroom with them, they cannot fast. But the days will come when the Bridegroom will be taken away from them, and then they will fast in those days."

If Lord Jesus is the Bridegroom, then it was no coincidence that His first miracle was at a wedding in Cana of Galilee (John 2:1-11). And truly if we look with Jewish eyes at the events of the Holy week, especially of Maundy, Thursday, and Good Friday, it appears to us that we are in front of a traditional Jewish wedding.

According to the Book of Revelation written with the inspiration of the Holy Spirit by St. John the Beloved –an earlier Jew- the whole world ends with an everlasting wedding:

"And I heard, as it were, the voice of a great multitude, as the sound of many waters and as the sound of mighty thunderings, saying, "Alleluia! For the Lord God Omnipotent reigns! Let us be glad and rejoice and give Him glory, for the marriage of the Lamb has come, and His wife has made herself ready." And to her, it was granted to be arrayed in fine linen, clean and bright, for the fine linen is the righteous acts of the saints. Then he said to me, write: 'Blessed are those who are called to the marriage supper of the Lamb!' And he said to me, "These are the true sayings of God." (Revelation 19:6-9)

And when the apostle John saw the wedding, he said:

"Then I, John, saw the holy city, New Jerusalem, coming down out of heaven from God, prepared as a bride adorned for her husband." (Revelation 21:2)

As portrayed above, we see that Lord Jesus Christ and St. John the Baptist along with St. John and St. Paul the apostles have all used the same simile. And when this allegory is repeated to this extent, its importance becomes clear. Hence, it is our turn to make more effort to understand it. Truly we won't be able to understand this simile unless we get back to the Jewish roots of Christianity.

The goal of the book is to take you back to the roots and to escort you on a journey to old Israel, in the days of Lord Jesus on earth. My objective is to introduce you to the Jewish wedding traditions at that time so you may see the greatness of this wonderful simile and great mystery.

This book aims to add a new perspective to the seven sacraments of the church, prayer, fasting, bible study and marriage. Overall, it intends to deepen your love for Jesus Christ and to strengthen your relationship with Him. It will help you acknowledge our glorified Lord not only as a creator and savior, but also as a loving Bridegroom in the heart of the history of salvation.

There's nothing more magnificent than this, for here is the Lord Himself following the footsteps of a Jewish Bridegroom, taking to Himself the church as the bride. Nonetheless, let us see how! Let us get back to the story from the beginning.

May The Lord use this book for the glory of His holy name through the prayers of His Holiness Pope Tawadros II, Pope of Alexandria and the Patriarch of the See of Saint Mark. Glory be to God forever and ever, Amen.

The author

Chapter 1

Jehovah Makes a Covenant with Israel

The true God "Jehovah"8 from the Jewish perspective is not only God the Creator but God of Israel, the Bridegroom. He is a God who always has a persistent desire to establish a living, deep, eternal, and sacrificial relationship with humans. This relationship originated on mount Sinai and it cannot be described but as a wedding between the creator and his creation, between God and man, between "Jehovah" and "Israel". This relationship is not merely a sacred covenant limited to the law of the ten commandments, but what happened on that mountain was truly a divine wedding. How did this relationship start and how did it develop?

The Beginning of the Covenant between the Bride and the Bridegroom

Exodus starts where Genesis ends. It speaks of God's interactions with His chosen people, thus it tracks a series of events from the migration of Jacob's sons to Egypt as guests of their brother Joseph who was of vast authority, until their redemption from the bonds of

---

8 In Hebrew יְהֹוָי - Yehôvâh, which is a word derived from the act of being הָיָה. It is one of God's names in the Old Testament as His revelation to the prophet Moses on Mount Horib, when he said to him: "Thus you shall say to the children of Israel: 'The Lord (Jehovah) God of your fathers, the God of Abraham, the God of Isaac, and the God of Jacob, has sent me to you. This is my name forever, and this is my memorial to all generations." (Exodus 3:15).

cruel slavery they were forced into by *"...a new king...who did not know Joseph" (Exodus 1:8)*

During the suppression of the Jews by the pharaoh, the prophet Moses appears as a deliverer for them and succeeds with the power of Jehovah, after the ten plagues, to free the twelve tribes of Israel from Egyptian slavery and the brutal pharaoh[9].

After celebrating the Passover and casting the pharaoh and his army into the Red Sea[10], Moses leads the tribes on a journey into the wilderness, borne on eagles' wings until they reach Mount Sinai. There, God the Creator of all existence reveals that He will appear on the mountain. To sanctify themselves to meet God on the mountain, the Lord ordered his people to wash their clothes (the wedding garment) and abstain from sexual relationships[11]. Then at last, in an unforgettable majestic appearance, God gives his people the Ten Commandments[12].

At this very moment, God started a very special relationship –the covenant[13]– with His people. This is what the divine revelation recorded regarding this wonderful covenant:

"And Moses wrote all the words of the Lord. And he rose early in the morning and built an altar at the foot of the mountain, and twelve pillars according to the twelve tribes of Israel. Then he sent young men of the children of Israel, who offered burnt offerings and sacrificed peace offerings of oxen to the Lord. And Moses took half the blood and put it in basins, and half the blood he sprinkled on the altar. Then he took the Book of the Covenant and read in the

---

9 (Exodus 1-3)

10 (Exodus 14,15)

11 (Ex. 19)

12 (Ex. 21)

13 In Hebrew, בְּרִית - berîyth, which means covenant, alliance, affinity, or commitment.

hearing of the people. And they said, "All that the Lord has said we will do, and be obedient." And Moses took the blood, sprinkled it on the people, and said, "This is the blood of the covenant which the Lord has made with you according to all these words. Then Moses went up, also Aaron, Nadab, and Abihu, and seventy of the elders of Israel, and they saw the God of Israel. And there was under His feet as it were a paved work of sapphire stone, and it was like the very heavens in its clarity. But on the nobles of the children of Israel He did not lay His hand. So they saw God, and they ate and drank." (Exodus 24: 4-11)

From a biblical perspective, the covenant is as a holy bond for people. It is of great importance in their lives as it builds a relationship that never splits. In this latter Exodus excerpt, we see how the relationship between the Bridegroom and His bride started off with an acceptance of the covenant's conditions/laws (the Ten Commandments), it then proceeded with worshiping God by offering sacrifices. Worshiping in this context is proclaiming one Bridegroom for the bride, she cannot have a relationship with or approach another to give worship.

Here, we see the twelve tribes entering into a holy relationship with God. This relationship is built after having sprinkled the blood on the altar (which represents the presence of God) and on the people. We are then before God the Creator and the Bridegroom who enters in a flesh and blood a relationship14 with His bride, the twelve tribes of Israel. This covenant reaches its fullness by celebrating a heavenly feast witnessed by Moses and the leaders, as they see the Bridegroom, eat and drink at the wedding feast.

---

14 And Adam said: "This is now bone of my bones and flesh of my flesh; she shall be called Woman, because she was taken out of Man." (Genesis 2: 23)

Reminding the Prophets of the Relationship of the Bridegroom with His bride

Mentioning the Bridegroom's relationship with the bride is not only confined to Exodus, but it appears in the other books of the prophets such as Isaiah, Jeremiah, Ezekiel and Hosea. These prophets saw a deeper mystery in what happened on Mount Sinai. They do not see it merely as a collection of statutory laws, but saw a spiritual engagement between God and Israel. Consequently, the God of Israel is not a creator only, but a Bridegroom as well, likewise they saw the twelve tribes of Israel gathered as a bride for God. Hosea recorded the words of God the Bridegroom talking about His bride Israel saying:

"Therefore, behold, I will allure her, Will bring her into the wilderness, and speak comfort to her.... She shall sing there, as in the days of her youth, As in the day when she came up from the land of Egypt." (Hosea 2:14-15).

And prophet Jeremiah said:

"Moreover, the word of the Lord came to me, saying, Go and cry in the hearing of Jerusalem, saying, thus says the Lord: I remember you, The kindness of your youth, The love of your betrothal, When you went after Me in the wilderness, In a land not sown." (Jeremiah 2:1,2)

Also, prophet Ezekiel said:

"When I passed by you again and looked upon you, indeed your time was the time of love; so, I spread My wing over you and covered your nakedness. Yes, I swore an oath to you and entered into a covenant with you, and you became Mine, says the Lord God." (Ezekiel 16:8)

Jehovah Makes a Covenant with Israel

Here we see the prophets Hosea, Jeremiah and Ezekiel parallelly indicate three important realities, as follows:

1. The three of them go back and look to the past, specifically to what happened in Exodus when the bride Israel got out from the land of Egypt, went into the wilderness, and made a covenant with God on Mount Sinai. These prophets were simply retelling the same story with its fine details.

2. The three of them show Israel as a bride in a covenant with her Bridegroom, who in order to take her as His fiance, allures her and calls her to the season of everlasting love.

3. The three of them clarify that the relationship between the Bridegroom and His bride is an ancient relationship and authenticated by a covenant.

Perhaps the mystery of the Bridegroom and His bride fades a little in the midst of sacrifices, laws and legislations of the Old Testament, but it appears plainly every now and then in the pages of the Old Testament to remind us of its presence and importance.

Certainly, the Jews understood this simile very well, that's why we find Rabbi Jose[15] when he was explaining the verse (Ex 19:17) *"And Moses brought the people out of the camp to meet with God, and they stood at the foot of the mountain."* Says: [The Lord came from Sinai to receive Israel, like a Bridegroom coming to meet His bride][16]

---

15 Jose ben Halafta: One of the most famous Jewish rabbis in the second century AD. He was a student of Rabbi Akiba and became a scholar of Talmudic jurisprudence and Jewish laws. He is mentioned prominently in the Mishnah, which contains many interpretations of the books of the Old Testament, being the fifth-most-frequently mentioned in it. Of the many Rabbi Yose's in the Talmud, Yose Ben Halafta is the one who is simply referred to as Rabbi Yose.

16 Mekilta de Rabbi-Ishmael/Trans. Jacob Z. Lauterbach: 3vols, Philadelphia, Jewish Publication Society of America, 1933, 2:218-19.

(Mekhilta on Exodus[17] 19:17)

Sin, Jealousy and Spiritual Adultery

Israel as a bride should remain loyal to her Bridegroom according to the laws of the covenant she pledged on mount Sinai. This explains that immorality, or as we call it spiritually "SIN" has a diverse meaning! Sin is not just disobeying the commandment but it is breaking the covenant as well. Thus, it is considered spiritual adultery, as it implies loving a stranger and being attached to someone else apart from the Bridegroom.

The bride is totally like a mirror that if set in a straight upright position before the rays of love flowing from her Bridegroom, she would reflect these rays and exchange love with Him, and no wonder, as her love is a reflection of His love to her. Nevertheless, if you set this mirror in an oblique position, the rays reflected from it deviate and reflect on someone else. Then this "OTHER" will be "GOD-LIKE" as the bride loves him with God's love, therefore this "OTHER" becomes a Lord and Master over her, and any love offered to the true God is considered fake. This makes the real Bridegroom ask His bride: "How do you say I love You and your heart is not with Me?" And that's why the bride is considered an adulteress.

The bride is honest:

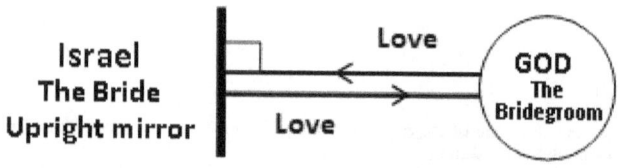

---

[17] Mekhilta on Exodus, meaning in Aramaic אתליכמ, meaning "base". It is a name given to the Midrash of the Book of Exodus because the interpretations and spiritual commentaries on the law in which they are found, are based on a fixed base, which is the criticism of the Jewish biblical text. Its author is not known for certain, but it is attributed to Rabbi Ishmael (Ismail), and the Jews consider it an important source of interpretation and legislation.

The bride is an adulteress:

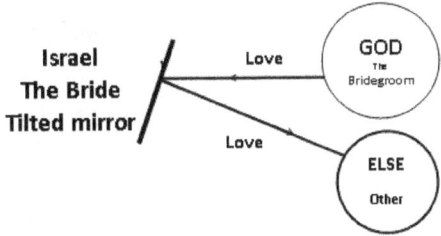

We must remember that Israel entered into a conditional relationship (the Ten Commandments), and in the first condition God says: *"You shall have no other gods before Me." (Exodus 20:3)*. When Israel worships another god other than "Jehovah", this means breaching the first term of her relationship contract with the Bridegroom. This way, she is breaking the connection with the Bridegroom and connecting to another. Unfortunately, that is what happened! From the books of the Old Testament, we see the bride committing spiritual adultery not long after her wedding ceremony.

According to the biblical narrative, after less than 40 days from the covenant on Mount Sinai, and without the knowledge of Prophet Moses, Aron and the leaders break the covenant with the God of Israel and offer a sacrifice to the golden calf as mentioned in Exodus 32:1-6:

"Now when the people saw that Moses delayed coming down from the mountain, the people gathered together to Aaron, and said to him, "Come, make us [a]gods that shall go before us; for as for this Moses, the man who brought us up out of the land of Egypt, we do not know what has become of him." And Aaron said to them, "Break off the golden earrings which are in the ears of your wives, your sons, and your daughters, and bring them to me." So all the people broke off the golden earrings which were in their ears, and brought them to Aaron. And he received the gold from their hand, and he fashioned it with an engraving tool, and made a molded

calf. Then they said, "This is your god, O Israel, that brought you out of the land of Egypt!" So when Aaron saw it, he built an altar before it. And Aaron made a proclamation and said, "Tomorrow is a feast to the Lord." Then they rose early on the next day, offered burnt offerings, and brought peace offerings; and the people sat down to eat and drink, and rose up to play."

This was the first instance of spiritual adultery by Israel, which was repeated many times across different generations. The people went astray and worshiped the false gods of the gentiles. This worship did not only include spiritual adultery but also physical prostitution and sexual rituals, and it even reached human sacrifices[18]. Yes, it may seem difficult to understand, from a modern perspective, how these sins were considered spiritual adultery, but we may be able to comprehend this fact if we looked back to the relationship between "Jehovah", the Bridegroom and Israel, the bride. We witness that adultery is committed every time the bride offers her love to anyone other than the Bridegroom. This is what the divine inspiration confirmed in many instances in the Old Testament, and clearly used the words "Harlot" and "Treacherous" to describe this state that the bride of Israel has reached. Here are some examples:

"Alas, sinful nation, A people laden with iniquity, A brood of evildoers, Children who are corrupters! They have forsaken the Lord, They have provoked to anger The Holy One of Israel, They have turned away backward.

"How the faithful city has become a harlot! It was full of justice; Righteousness lodged in it, But now murderers." (Isaiah 1:4,21)

"Can a virgin forget her ornaments, Or a bride her attire? Yet My people have forgotten Me days without number. Surely, as a wife treacherously departs from her husband, So have you dealt

---

[18] See for example (Numbers 25), (Judges 11), (1 Kings 11), (2 Kings 15-17) and (2 Kings 24,25).

Jehovah Makes a Covenant with Israel

treacherously with Me, O house of Israel," says the Lord." (Jeremiah 2:32 and 3:20)

Nevertheless, her Bridegroom is "Jealous" and the Holy Bible has clearly mentioned that six times[19]. The Hebrew word "Zealous" that is always used is אָנֵק - qannâ' - kan-naw', derived from the word אנק. This is the same word used to describe a man's jealousy for his wife in the Bible[20]. For example in (Num 5:30): "or when the spirit of jealousy comes upon a man, and he becomes jealous (אָנֵק - qannâ' - kan-naw') of his wife; then he shall stand the woman before the Lord...".

Unfortunately, the bride was never satisfied with her cheating but she went too far in her offense and took the Bridegroom's precious gifts and offered them to strangers, to other gods. Regarding this, the divine inspiration speaks through the prophet Ezekiel:

"But you trusted in your own beauty, played the harlot because of your fame, and poured out your harlotry on everyone passing by who would have it. You took some of your garments and adorned multicolored high places for yourself, and played the harlot on them. Such things should not happen, nor be. You have also taken your beautiful jewelry from My gold and My silver, which I had given you, and made for yourself male images and played the harlot with them. You took your embroidered garments and covered them, and you set My oil and My incense before them. Also My food which I gave you—the pastry of fine flour, oil, and honey which I fed you—you set it before them as sweet incense; and so it was," says the Lord God. "Moreover you took your sons and your daughters, whom you bore to Me, and these you sacrificed to them

---

[19] See (Exodus 20:5), twice in (Exodus 34:14), (Deuteronomy 4:24), (Deuteronomy 5:9) and (Deuteronomy 6:15).

[20] Francis Brown, S. R. Driver and Charles A. Briggs: Brown- Driver- Briggs Hebrew and English Lexicon with an appendix containing the Biblical Aramaic, Enhanced Edition, 2000, P 159.

to be devoured. Were your acts of harlotry a small matter, that you have slain My children and offered them up to them by causing them to pass through the fire? And in all your abominations and acts of harlotry you did not remember the days of your youth, when you were naked and bare, struggling in your blood." (Ezekiel 16:15-22) (NKJV) This is why her real husband describes her as Adulterous saying: *"You are an adulterous wife, who takes strangers instead of her husband." (Ezekiel 16:32)*

To picture this state, "Jehovah" used a practical example that may seem odd, perhaps His bride may return to her senses, turn back and repent. He commanded prophet Hosea saying: *"... Go, take yourself a wife of harlotry And children of harlotry, For the land has committed great harlotry By departing from the Lord. So he went and took Gomer the daughter of Diblaim, and she conceived and bore him a son." (Hosea 1:2-3)*

Here prophet Ezekiel represents God, whilst his wife Gomer represents Israel and we stand before a symbolic image explaining how God's people became as an adulterous bride to her heavenly Bridegroom[21].

The sin of the bride Israel was magnified as she repeatedly broke her commitment to keep the covenant with her Bridegroom. These commitments that she pledged to keep when she received the 10 commandments when all the people said: *" ... All that the Lord has spoken we will do ... "(Exodus 19:8)*

In his comment on this verse, one of the ancient rabbis[22] said in

---

[21] See also, "Thus says the Lord: "Where is the certificate of your mother's divorce, Whom I have put away? Or which of My creditors is it to whom I have sold you? For your iniquities you have sold yourselves, and for your transgressions your mother has been put away". (Isiah 50 :1) and "Then I saw that for all the causes for which backsliding Israel had committed adultery, I had put her away and given her a certificate of divorce; yet her treacherous sister Judah did not fear, but went and played the harlot also". (Jeremiah 3 :8)

[22] Rabbis: The plural of Rabbi. In Hebrew רַבִּי, it means "master" or "teacher". In this book, we preferred to use the word "rabbi" because it is the most commonly used, and by it we mean the reference to Jewish jurists who interpreted the written books and explained the

the Midrash of Deuteronomy: [God married Israel to Himself when the people pledged to say: "All that the Lord has spoken, we will do", but when they made the golden calf, Moses told them: "you haven't kept the covenant..."]23.

Renewing the Covenant

Despite the frequent stumbling of the bride Israel and her betrayal of her heavenly Bridegroom, her Bridegroom never abandoned her. On the contrary, He stayed faithful despite her unfaithfulness. This loving Bridegroom was looking forward to the day when the bride shall wake up from her wine and get back to Him. He was waiting for that day when she repents to forgive her sins and establish a new marriage covenant with her.

That is why in the books of the prophets, we find a wonderful conversation concerning the reconciliation between God and His unfaithful Bride. We see the prophets speaking about a new covenant between God and his distant bride, and these are some examples:

Prophet Hosea says: "... She shall sing there, As in the days of her youth, As in the day when she came up from the land of Egypt. "And it shall be, in that day," Says the Lord, "That you will call Me 'My Husband', And no longer call Me 'My Master,' For I will take from her mouth the names of the Baals, And they shall be remembered by their name no more. In that day I will make a covenant for them ... I will betroth you to Me forever; Yes, I will betroth you to Me In righteousness and justice, In loving kindness and mercy; I will betroth you to Me in faithfulness, And you shall know the Lord." (Hosea 2:15-20)

---

oral tradition. In modern Judaism, the Rabbi is a person qualified by academic studies of the Hebrew Bible and the Talmud to act as spiritual leader and religious teacher of a Jewish community or congregation.

23 Michael L. Satlow: Jewish marriagr between God and Israel, Princeton University Press, 2001, P 54.

Prophet Isaiah says: *"For your Maker is your husband, The Lord of hosts is His name ... For the Lord has called you Like a woman forsaken and grieved in spirit, Like a youthful wife when you were refused," Says your God. "For a mere moment I have forsaken you, But with great mercies I will gather you. With a little wrath I hid My face from you for a moment; But with everlasting kindness I will have mercy on you," Says the Lord, your Redeemer. For the mountains shall depart And the hills be removed, But My kindness shall not depart from you, Nor shall My covenant of peace be removed," Says the Lord, who has mercy on you."* (Isaiah 54:5-8,10)

And prophet Jeremiah says: *"Behold, the days are coming, says the Lord, when I will make a new covenant with the house of Israel and with the house of Judah— not according to the covenant that I made with their fathers in the day that I took them by the hand to lead them out of the land of Egypt, My covenant which they broke, [h]though I was a husband to them, says the Lord. But this is the covenant that I will make with the house of Israel after those days, says the Lord: I will put My law in their minds, and write it on their hearts; and I will be their God, and they shall be My people. No more shall every man teach his neighbor, and every man his brother, saying, 'Know the Lord,' for they all shall know Me, from the least of them to the greatest of them, says the Lord. For I will forgive their iniquity, and their sin I will remember no more."* (Jeremiah 31:31-34)

Prophet Ezekiel says: *"Nevertheless I will remember My covenant with you in the days of your youth, and I will establish an everlasting covenant with you. And I will establish My covenant with you. Then you shall know that I am the Lord, that you may remember and be ashamed, and never open your mouth anymore because of your shame, when I provide you an atonement for all you have done,"* says the Lord God." (Ezekiel 16:60,62,63)

Jehovah Makes a Covenant with Israel

Here is a great hope for the people of Israel for a new relationship with God. We notice throughout the previous prophecies that every time God gives his people a new covenant, this covenant is a marriage vow, where God overflows with his numerous loving gifts of justice, righteousness, kindness[24], and mercy[25] over his bride as said by prophet Hosea.

We also notice that this new covenant is initially concerned with forgiving the sins of Israel. Here, the bride broke the relationship which started in her early days after escaping from Egypt. Despite all of that, God promises to forgive all the sins she committed. God the Bridegroom addresses Israel when prophet Hosea said: "You (Israel) will call Me 'My Husband[26]', And no longer call Me 'My Master'[27]".

This means that the bride will call "Jehovah" Man (husband) not Baal (Master). God gently speaks to His bride saying: "In the past, my bride, you used to consider the gods of the gentiles as your masters but in the future, you shall call me the Lord, your only Bridegroom. For I am not only a master to you but I am also your loving Bridegroom.

The redemption of Israel, the bride, will not occur only through the forgiveness of her sins, but when she accepts her Bridegroom. For here, God declares that He is not a distant God, but he is a true Bridegroom who wants His bride to know Him and enter a relationship that is not only fruitful or faithful but also eternal[28].

---

24 In the Hebrew origin, חֶסֶד means good, kindness, or devotion.

25 In the Hebrew origin, רחם meaning compassion, and this word is so beautiful as it is also used to mean a woman's womb, as if the one who offers mercy is like a mother who protects a child in her womb from the cruelty of the world. See מחַ in Brown–Driver–Briggs/A Hebrew and English Lexicon of the OT.

26 From the Hebrew שיא which means husband.

27 From the Hebrew יְלעַב meaning master.

28 From the Hebrew עֲלֹם עַד, which means eternity or perpetual over time.

Therefore, we can conclude that human history over the entirety of the Old Testament is considered an eternal love story in which we see all the realistic fine details of the relationship between the Bridegroom and His bride. In it we see love, sincerity, tenderness, treachery on behalf of the bride, mercy, forgiveness and renewal of the vows.

One of the ancient rabbis said in his comment on Exodus Midrash *[This world is the betrothal as He says "I will betroth you to Me in faithfulness, And you shall know the Lord." (Hosea 2:20) ... but the wedding will be in the days of the Messiah as He says "For your Maker is your husband" (Isaiah 54:5)]* [29]

---

[29] Rabbi Dr. H. Freedman & Maurice Simon: Midrash Rabbah/Exodus, The Soncino Press, 1961, P 204.

Chapter 2

Love in the Song of Songs

In the book of the Song of Songs "Jehovah", the Loving Bridegroom chooses to pour out all of His heart toward his beloved bride.

Skeptics see the Song of Songs only as a collection of flirtatious poems between a husband and a wife, while many see it as a symbolic story between God, the Bridegroom and the human soul, the bride.

Nevertheless, we must clarify that according to the ancient tradition, Jews never understood the Song of Songs in either way because they considered it as a figurative story expressing **the love of God, the Bridegroom to His bride, Israel.**

The Jewish Perspective of the Book

In Hebrew, it is called שׁיר30 שירים (Shir Hashirim) and it is considered one of their canonical books, for that reason, the Jews consider it as holy and add it to the books of "Tanakh" (the Jewish Holy Bible) along with four other books which are Ruth, Lamentations, Ecclesiastes, and Esther. They call them "The Five Megillot" תולigמ שמח and put them in the third section of the divine books after the Torah and the Prophets.

---

30 שׁיר: A word which means a religious song, anthem, or a hymn. It is generally used during times of victory and thanksgiving like the praise that the prophet Moses and the children of Israel praised after their salvation from the Pharaoh in (Exodus 15:1), the praise of Israel at the well in (Deuteronomy 21: 17), the praise of Deborah in (Judges 5: 12). In the New Testament, the praise of the virgin Mary in (Luke 1:46) and the twenty-four priests in (Revelation 5:9).

Nowadays, the "Ashkenazim"[31] Jews read it on Saturdays and on the Sabbath of Passover, but the "Sephardic"[32] Jews recite it every Friday night[33]. In the first century AD, Josephus the Historian[34] added the Song of Songs to the group of poetry books that contain what he called "The Songs of God".[35]

To prove its authenticity, it is always important to look into the quotes cited from a book. The book of Hosea quotes from the book of the Songs of Songs in "I will be like the dew to Israel; He shall grow like the lily, And lengthen his roots like Lebanon." (Hosea 14:5) which is quoted from (Song 2:2) I am the rose of Sharon, And the lily of the valleys.".

Correspondingly, the Fourth Esdras book[36] uses an image from the Song of Songs to describe the relationship between God and His beloved city Jerusalem saying: And I said, Oh Sovereign YAHWEH that bears rule, of every wood of the earth, and of all the trees thereof, YOU have chosen for YOURSELF only one vine: And of all lands of the whole world YOU have chosen for YOURSELF one region: and of all the flowers of the world YOU

---

31 Ashkenazi Jews: In Hebrew: מִינְזְכַשׁא . They are the Jews of Eastern European descent.

32 The Sephardic Jews: In Hebrew: תודהי דרפס. They are descended of the Jews who were expelled from Spain and Portugal in the fifteenth and sixteenth centuries, then they settled in the Mediterranean basin, the Balkans and some other regions. It is worth noting that there are also the Mizrahi Jews, the oriental Jews in the literal meaning or the Jews of the Middle East.

33 The unedited full-text of the 1906 Jewish Encyclopedia Interpretation, 2002-2011, Jewish Encyclopedia / Song of Songs.

34 Josephus: His name is Joseph Ben Matthias, and in Hebrew: יוסִפ בֶ והיתתמ. He was a scholar and biographer who lived in the first century AD. He chronicled many important events in the Jewish history, especially the first Jewish-Roman war (66-73 AD). He died in 100 AD at the age of 63.

35 William Whiston & Paul L. Maier: The new complete work of Josephus, Kregel Production, 1999, P 939.

36 Esdras IV: It is an uncanonical book consisting of visions that Ezra has seen in the captivity, thirty years after the Babylonians destroyed Jerusalem. The theme of these visions is how a just and loving God can allow His people to suffer this grief. It is not considered canonical by the Christians. However, it is known as one of the important Jewish books that talk about the end of the world. It can be relied not as a canonical prophetic book inspired by the Holy Spirit, but only as a book from which we explore Jewish history and customs.

have chosen for YOURSELF one lily. (Quoted from the Song of Songs 2:2 "Like a lily among thorns, So is my love among the daughters."). And from all the depths of the sea YOU have filled for YOURSELF one river: and of all built cities YOU have set it apart and made kodesh Zion to YOURSELF. (EZRA -4- ESDRAS 5:23 – 25).[37]

The Jewish Rabbis have looked to the book in a figurative way, Rabbi Akiva[38] considered the book as one of the most sacred Jewish books. He said: [The one who warbles their voice when they recite the Song of Songs when they are in a feasting hall and makes it like a song has no share in the world to come.][39] (Tosefta Sanhedrin 12:10)[40]

He also said: [For the whole world is not as worthy as the day on which the Song of Songs was given to Israel; for all the writings are holy but the Song of Songs is the holy of holies.][41])Mishnah Yadayim 3:5)[42]

---

37 The Old Testament Pseudepigrapha/volume 1/Apocalyptic Literature and Testaments, Fourth Book of Ezra, Doubleday & Company inc., 1983, P 533.

38 Rabbi Akiva: His name in Hebrew is יוֹסֵף בַּ אֲבִיקְעַ and is also called "Akiba". He lived between 50 and 135 AD and is one of the rabbis who contributed a great role in writing the Mishnah and Midrash. The Talmud calls him the chief of the wise. He was executed by the Romans following one of the Jews' revolts against Roman rule.

39 Goldwurm, Hersh, Nosson Scherman, Yisroel S. Schorr, and Chaim Malinowitz. Talmud Bavli: [talmud Bavli] : the Schottenstein Edition : the Gemara : the Classic Vilna Edition, with an Annotated, Interpretive elucidation, As an Aid to Talmud Study. , 1990. Print. Sanhedrin 101a.

40 The Sanhedrin or Tosefta Sanhedrin is a body of oral Jewish statutes and laws from the 2nd century CE. It is considered an annex to the Mishnah. The Sanhedrin is a name given by the Jews during the period of the incarnation of Lord Jesus to the Supreme Court of the Jewish nation, and it was the official representative for the Jewish people before the Romans. The Sanhedrin consisted of seventy-one members, seventy of whom were like the number of elders who helped Moses, and the seventy-first was the chief priest or the high priest, and in general the Sanhedrin had the right to legislate in religious, political and social rulings. But it stopped working after the year 70 AD, after the destruction of Jerusalem and the Jewish diaspora.

41 Philip Blackman: Mishnayoth Volume VI/Order Taharoth, Judaica Press, Second Edition, 1977, P 764.

42 Mishnah Yadayim: Mishnah or the Mishnah, in Hebrew הנשמב, a word derived from the Hebrew verb "; Shannah" Its meaning in Arabic (to commend or repeat) is a word that refers specifically to the study of oral law, which is the first written in the Oral Torah, and

Rabbi Akiva means that whoever looks to the book as a merely traditional romantic song makes a huge mistake as this book is not defiled or has any unholy desire, it represents the Holy of Holies. It is a love relationship springing out of the Holy God. As for Rabbi Akiva, the Bridegroom of the book is "The one who said Be, and the world Was" (the creator) and the Bride is "Israel"[43].

Maybe not all the Old Jewish Rabbis have the same perspective as Rabbi Akiva, but most of them (Especially in the Midrash and Targum) understood the book in its' figurative meaning, as an image describing the relationship between God the Bridegroom and His covenant with His Bride Israel[44]. The Rabbis interpreted it allegorically as a wedding between "Jehovah", the lover Who appears in the book as a shepherd and the children of Israel, His beloved, who appears in the book as a countryside girl[45].

The Song's Bridegroom and Bride

There were strict laws of the Kings regarding women mentioned in Deuteronomy: "When you come to the land which the Lord your God is giving you, and possess it and dwell in it, and say, 'I will set a king over me like all the nations that are around me,' you shall surely set a king over you whom the Lord your God chooses; one from among your brethren you shall set as king over you; you may not set a foreigner over you, who is not your brother. Neither shall he multiply wives for himself, lest his heart turns away; nor shall he greatly multiply silver and gold for himself." (Deut 17:14,15,17).

---

includes legislation and a wide range of commentaries and interpretations that deal with the books of the Old Testament and are considered the most important sources on the Jewish tradition, and the word Yadayim means hands It is Mishna on the ritual purification of the hands of Jewish rabbis.

43 Jacob Z. Lauterbach: Mekilta de- Rabbi Ishmael, Volume 3, The Jewish Publication Society of America, 1935, 3: P 49-63.

44 The unedited full-text of the 1906 Jewish Encyclopedia Interpretation, 2002-2011/ Solomon as Bridegroom.

45 Philip and Hanna Goodman: The Jewish Marriage anthology, The Jewish Publication Society of America, 1971, P 11.

*However, we see King Solomon marrying women more than all the kings of Israel, as it is mentioned in "And he had seven hundred wives, princesses, and three hundred concubines... " (1 Kings 11:3). Therefore, some may wonder: **Why can't the Song of Songs be a description of one of King Solomon's thousand marriages?***

To answer this question, we need to take a closer look at the Bridegroom. We must ask if the characteristics of the Bridegroom in the Song of Songs apply to King Solomon or if they are the characteristics of the God of Israel. The truth is, when we study the Old Testament books, we clearly see that the characteristics and designations describing the Bridegroom in the song are typically the ones used to describe the God of Israel. Surely when we do the comparison in the Hebrew language, it would be further clarified. That is why we made it a point to add the original Hebrew word beside its English counterpart to understand the extent of their compatibility, which appears in the table below:

Compatibilities	The God of Israel in the Testaments	The groom in the book of Song of Songs	Comments	Reflection
Loving God and loving the Bridegroom	" Hear, O Israel: The Lord our God, the Lord is one! You shall love (בהא) the Lord your God with all your heart, with all your soul(נפשׁ) and with all your strength." (Deuteronomy 6: 4,5)	" O you whom my soul (נפשׁ) love (אהב) " (Song of songs 1:7, 3:1,2,3,4)	Both Hebrew origins use the same two words (love and soul) and they are repeated in the same order	O Israel, you must love your Lord not only as God, but also as a soul-loving Bridegroom. As your God is one, so your Bridegroom is one, so love for Him must be with all the soul and all the strength.

Christ the Bridegroom

Joy on the day of God and joy in meeting the Bridegroom	" This *is* the day the Lord has made; We will rejoice(גִיל) and be glad(שָׂמֵחַ) in it. (psalm 118:24)	" The king has brought me into his chambers.. We will be glad(גִיל) and rejoice (שָׂמַח) in you". (Song of songs 1:4)	The words glad and rejoice are used and are repeated in the same order	The meeting of the Bridegroom is not just a day (with a as an article), but it is the day (defined with THE). It is not like any other day because it is a special day. The day of joy and happiness.
God is the shepherd and the Bridegroom is the shepherd	" The Lord is my shepherd(רָעָה); I shall not want. He makes me to lie down (רָבַץ) in green pastures;" (psalm 23:1,2)	"Tell me, O you whom I love, Where you feed your flock(רָעָה), Where you make it rest(רָבַץ) at noon. (Song of songs 1:7)	The words shepherd/ shepherds and lie down are used and are repeated in the same order	Your Bridegroom is also your Shepherd. He feels your fatigue, and He is the wise administrator who comforts you from the noon heat of the of this world.
Desirable God and sweet Bridegroom	" The fear of the Lord is clean, enduring forever; The judgments of the Lord are true and righteous altogether. More to be desired(חָמַד) are they than gold, Yea, than much fine gold; (psalm 19:9,10)	"His mouth *is* most sweet, Yes, he is altogether lovely. (מַחֲמָד)" (song of song 5:16)	The word desired מַחֲמָד, which appears in Song 5:16, is derived from the Hebrew word חָמַד, which appears in Psalm 19:9,10	The Bridegroom's mouth is most sweet, as His mouth pronounces the rulings of truth and justice.

It should be noted that there are a multitude of words and images concerning the God of Israel mentioned in the Old Testament books which correspond to the Bridegroom described in the Song

Love in the Song of Songs

of Songs, but these few examples were used to illustrate the idea.

The Bridegroom in the Jewish Prayers

In their attempt to save the Jews surviving the death camps46 in Europe, some rabbis from the United States traveled to France in 1945 to try to find survivors. They found out there were some Jewish children in a remote monastery in southern France. Therefore, they immediately decided to travel to this monastery and when they arrived, they found many children, but the abbot in charge refused to hand over any of the children without official papers testifying that these children were Jews.

At this point, the situation got worse as there were many children from different religious backgrounds and there was no way to discern the Jewish children from the others. However, one of the rabbis had a smart idea and he asked if the rabbis could return in the evening at bedtime and the abbot agreed. As agreed upon, the rabbis returned in the evening, entered the dormitory, and found the children on their beds preparing to sleep. The rabbis shouted out loud at once "Shima Yisrael"[47], and here all the Jewish children covered their eyes out of fear because of what they suffered in the camps since 1939 as they were afraid to hear any Jewish prayers. Through this idea, the Jewish children were identified and handed over to the rabbis to be taken care of[48].

---

46 Death camps: It is a word given by the Jews to the camps set up by the Nazis in the stir of Hitler's seizure of power in 1933 AD. Until the end of World War II, 22 major concentration camps were established in Europe in addition to hundreds of camps in which thousands of Jews suffered from forced labor, ill-treatment, starvation, disease and random executions.

47 Shema Yisrael: in Hebrew שְׁמַע יִשְׂרָאֵל, which means "Hear, O Israel." They are the first two words in a phrase taken from the fourth verse of the sixth chapter of Deuteronomy, which says "Hear, O Israel: The Lord our God, the Lord is one." It is known as the Shema and it occupies the main part in the morning and evening prayers of the Jews. It is very revered by the Jews until now, as they consider it to carry the essence of the Jewish religion by acknowledging the oneness of God.

48 Based on a story told by Rabbi Yacov Barber in one of his lectures on the power of the Shema prayer. Check out Rabbibarber.com

The previous table and this story clarify the importance of the "Shima prayer" to the Jews as they pray it every morning and evening. We see in it a divine order for Israel to love God as a sole Bridegroom who is deserving of love from all the heart, all the soul, and all the strength. This is what the Jews acknowledge in their prayer of the shepherd psalm (psalm 23), where the Bridegroom appears as the shepherd Who nurtures His bride Israel, so she shall not want. In addition to Psalm 118 which is prayed in different celebrations and Jewish ceremonies, all these prayers identically describe the Bridegroom in the Song of Songs as mentioned earlier.

The Song of Songs is then reusing a collection of images and terms mentioned in other books of the Old Testament, presented by king Solomon in a poetic manner reflecting the relationship between God the Bridegroom and Israel His bride. The Jews in king Solomon's time understood it in the same sense due to their knowledge of the biblical terms and expressions[49].

Finally, after many attempts on behalf of the Bridegroom with this bride, the Bridegroom came, driven by His love and was incarnate. He became man, so the bride Israel examined Him. She saw Him as a Bridegroom who teaches her, satiates her, heals her and revives her from death. But *"He came to His own, and His own did not receive Him." (John 1:11).* Let us see then what the Bridegroom has done!

---

[49] Ellen F. Davis: Proverbs, Ecclesiastes, and the Song of Songs, Westminister Bible Compaanion, 2000, P 231.

Chapter 3

Christ Betroths the Bride

Christ, the Church's Bridegroom

Have you ever seen a bride crucifying her Bridegroom? Yes, she is Israel who betrayed her Bridegroom's covenant and returned His love with hatred.

After Israel's rejection of Her Bridegroom, Christ the incarnate Son of God, the Bible tells us about a new marriage covenant established by Christ. This time it is different. This new covenant is not only for the Jews but for the gentiles as well. In this light, this chapter will examine the Jewish marriage traditions at the time of our Lord Jesus, in an attempt to understand the new covenant in a deeper manner.

First of all, we need to know that marriage holds a special place in Judaism. Out of all the Jewish rituals, nothing is more joyful than marriage. It is considered the most elated celebration (in Hebrew הָשִׂמְחָ- Simcha) of all50. Therefore, it is normal that we see the Talmud rabbis discussing the topic of marriage on a wide range. The third part of the Talmud is called "Nashim" which means "Women". Among its seven sections, we find long articles on "Yevamot", meaning "The brothers and sisters of the couple", "Ketubot" which means "Marriage contracts", "Gittin" referring

---
50 Barney Kadsan: God's Appointed Customs/ A Messianic Jewish Guide to the Biblical Lifecycle and Lifestyle, Messianic Jewish Publishers, 1996, P 48.

to "Divorce laws" and "Kiddushin" which is "Engagement". Nevertheless, all these topics are found distributed and fragmented across other parts of the Talmud.

The Jews believe that the first couple, Adam and Eve, had marriage rituals that have never been repeated across subsequent ages as God Himself is the One Who beautified the bride Eve before bringing her to Adam. According to the Midrash, God ordered the angels saying: "Let's do a loving favor to Adam and his wife because the whole world is set on favors of love, and they please Me more than the sacrifices which the sons of Israel shall offer on the altar". So the angels were made present and surrounded the couple, and God blessed them, then the angels played hymns.

Concerning the first wedding in human history, Adam and Eve's wedding, Genesis mentions *"And Adam said: This is now bone of my bones and flesh of my flesh; She shall be called Woman, because she was taken out of Man."* (Genesis 2:23)

The Midrash clarifies that Adam gave Eve, after her creation, the name of "woman" which is אִשָּׁה - ishshâh in Hebrew as she was taken from "man" which is אִישׁ - îysh in Hebrew. The reason behind these names is that God has put His Name's Hebrew letters (יְהוָֹה – Jehovah) in the names of man and woman. He gave the man the letter "יְ - Yodh" and gave the woman the letter "ה - hei" to explain that as long as the couple walks in the way of God and keeps His commandments, they will be kept in His name with no evil. However, if they walk away from Him, His name's letters will be taken away from them. And instead of (אִישׁ and אִשָּׁה), the only letters left will be (אֵשׁ - êsh) which means "fire" in Hebrew. The fire that exits each of them to burn the other[51].

Naturally, Jewish marriage rituals have evolved since Adam and

---

51 Philip and Hanna Goodman: The Jewish Marriage anthology, The Jewish Publication Society of America, 1971, P 24 & 34.

Christ Betroths the Bride

Eve's marriage, but the traditional Jewish marriage remained divided into two main parts throughout history. These parts are **"Engagement" and "Marriage"**. Both were preserved with specific steps that may either merge together or divide according to the circumstances of the couple.

We will talk about the steps of the engagement in details in this chapter. The Hebrew word used to describe the engagement is וְיסוּרִיא Erosin. There is another word that is also used which is וְיִשׁוּדִיק "Kedoshin" that means "sanctification" or "holiness" as it comes from the word שׁוֹדָק "Kadosh" that means "Holy"[52] and it is one of God's characteristics in the Old Testament. The God of the Jews has raised the value of marriage to be a holy state. He offered Himself as a vital partner in this relationship. He is the cornerstone of the definition of holy marriage. The word engaged also has the same Hebrew origin, it is "תשדוקמ" - Mekdeshit which means "sacred/holy" but the woman even if she was engaged, she is still a human. Who can sanctify her except the holy God of Israel?! God, here, truly is a main partner of the marriage[53].

The engagement may reach up to 12 months before the actual marriage takes place. It includes a covenant. In fact, engagement in the Jewish tradition differs from its modern-day counterpart. It had a greater feeling of commitment on account of a covenant to be made. In fact, covenants in ancient times were serious, important, final, documented, and implied a legal obligation, one which was not easily breakable. Once the two parties enter the engagement covenant, they become like a married couple in everything except

---

[52] Revise "And one cried to another and said: "Holy, holy, holy is the Lord of hosts; The whole earth is full of His glory!" (Isaiah 6:3)

[53] This rather applies in Christian marriage. Marriage in Christianity is a holy sacrament where God is present as a third party, bringing together the two parties and sanctifying the relationship. He is the Holy Spirit Who unites them to become one. "So then, they are no longer two but one flesh. Therefore, what God has joined together, let not man separate." (Matthew 19:6).

in physical intercourse[54]. The engaged/betrothed woman had the same status as her married counterparts. That is why she would be widowed after the death of her fiancé. She has all the financial rights of a married woman if she is widowed or divorced. If she betrays her fiancé, she falls under the same judgment as an unfaithful wife[55]. As a betrothed, her fiancé cannot leave her without writing her a bill of divorce[56].

Since our Lord is the Bridegroom which makes a new marriage covenant, **He took the same footsteps of the Jewish Bridegroom taking to Himself the church as His bride.**

Unfortunately, many of these footsteps disappear because they are not seen from a Jewish perspective. When we study the traditions and the rituals of the Jewish marriage, we can see Christ the Bridegroom and the church His bride in every step. Let us examine these steps, but before that, my dear reader I need you to be prepared to be a bride for Christ! I urge you to echo the prophet Isaiah saying:

*"I will greatly rejoice in the Lord, my soul shall be joyful in my God; For He has clothed me with the garments of salvation, He has covered me with the robe of righteousness, As a **Bridegroom** decks himself with ornaments, And as a **bride** adorns herself with her jewels." (Isaiah 61:10).*

---

54 We note that the blessed Virgin Mary was betrothed to Saint Joseph the carpenter." Now the birth of Jesus Christ was as follows: After His mother Mary was betrothed to Joseph, before they came together, she was found with child of the Holy Spirit. "(Matthew 1:18).

55 "Then Joseph her husband, being a just man, and not wanting to make her a public example, was minded to put her away secretly." (Matthew 1:19).

56 W.L. Strack & P.L. Billenbeck: Kommentar Zum Neuen Testamentaus Talmud und Midrash, Munchen, 1924, vol. 2, P 277-394.

Step 1: Choosing the Bride

There is a humorous story[57] told in the Talmud[58] about Rabbi Jose ben Halafta. A Roman lady who was married to one of the nobles came to Rabbi Jose and asked: "What has been your God doing since He completed the creation of the world?" The Rabbi answered her: "He matches husbands to wives", but she sarcastically denounced this: "Is this considered a deed? Even I can do that! I have many servants for whom I am a matchmaker". The Rabbi answered: "It may seem easy to you, but it is as complicated as the splitting of the Red Sea!" The Roman lady was not convinced. Early in the morning, she gathered all her servants, men, and women, and started pointing to one of her male servants ordering him to marry this maid, commanding one of her maids to marry another servant, and so on until all her male and female servants were coupled. However, with the first beam of light the next morning, all the people she had matched came to her, one with a broken skull, the other missing an eye. One had an ear cut off, and the other, a broken leg. Someone shouted, "I don't want this woman," and another said, "I can't stand this man."

---

[57] Rabbi Maurice Lamm: The Jewish Way in Love & Marriage, Jonathan David Publishers, inc, 2008, P 3.

[58] Talmud: דּוּמְלַת in Hebrew a name means "teaching". It is the central text of Rabbinic Judaism and the primary source of Jewish religious law (halakha) and Jewish theology. It is divided into two parts "Mishnah" which is the subject and "Gemara"; which is the explanation. The Mishnah that means repetition is a collection of different Jewish traditions with some verses from the Bible. The Jews claim that these traditions were given to Moses when he was on the mountain, then Aaron, Eliezer, and Joshua circulated them and handed them over to the prophets. After that they were passed on from the prophets to the members of the Great Synagogue and their successors until the second century after Christ when Rabbi Judah compiled and wrote them. Then this person became for them the collector of the Mishnah. As for the "Gemara", it is a collection of debates, teachings and interpretations that took place in the higher schools after the end of the Mishnah. The commentaries written with the Mishnah are of two types The first is known as the Talmud of Jerusalem, which was written between the third and fifth centuries, and those who wrote it are the Rabbis of Tiberias, and the second is known as the Talmud of Babylon, which was written in the fifth century. The Talmud helps us a lot in studying the teachings of Christ, as it explains some of the symbols and similes contained in them, such as washing hands and others. The Lord Christ said to the Pharisees that they make the word of God of no effect through their tradition (Mark 7: 1 - 13).

The Talmud recounts that this noble lady came back to Rabbi Jose and said to him: "You were right". The Talmud comments on this story and says: "Matchmaking of couples seemed a trivial matter in the eyes of that woman, but it is not for God. This woman did not understand the basics of the difference between human personalities and the difficulty of making one stranger fit in with another."[59]

It is also mentioned in the Talmud that forty days before the birth of a child, a voice shouts in the heaven: "The son of this person will marry the daughter of so-and-so"[60]. Of course, finding the right person for marriage is a divine mission.

How did the Bridegroom Choose His bride in the Old Days?

1. In old Israel, the bridegroom's father was the one who chose his son's bride. Usually, he sent one of his faithful servants to look for a suitable bride. The best example of this can be found in Genesis 24: 2-9, where we read about Abraham sending his most trusted servant "Eliezer of Damascus" whose name means "my God is help" [61] to find a wife for his son Isaac. Eliezer succeeded in his mission and found the bride, Rebecca[62].

---

[59] Resolutely seeking God's guidance in marriage is important to its success. It is God who reconciles between the two parties, so that each party takes its partner from God's hand. That is why we see in the Bible, Eliezer of Damascus, who prayed five times before he betrothed to Rebekah to Isaac. There are many verses in the Bible that explain God's role in choosing. For example, at the marriage of Rebekah, Bethuel and Laban her brother said: "The thing comes from the Lord; we cannot speak to you either bad or good". (Genesis 24:50). Moreover, the Book of the Proverbs says that "Houses and riches are an inheritance from fathers, But a prudent wife is from the Lord. (Proverbs 19:14).

[60] Ari L. Goldman: Being Jewish, The Spiritual and Cultural Practice of Judaism Today, Simon & Schuster Paperback, 2000, P 69

[61] Eliezer: In Hebrew, הֱזְעִילָא is a compound word of two words, לְא EL, means God/God, and הֱזְע ' ezer, means help/assistance. The meaning of his name is the God of help or the God of assistance.

[62] Barney Kadsan: God's Appointed Customs/ A Messianic Jewish Guide to the Biblical Lifecycle and Lifestyle, Messianic Jewish Publishers, 1996, P 48.

The role played by "Eliezer the Damascus" became known afterward by the name "Shadkhan", known in English as the "Matchmaker".[63] [64]

Naturally, the bridegroom's father would make his greatest effort to find the best bride for his son. The bridegroom also used to participate in the choosing process if he was mature enough or according to the circumstances. But in general, the traditions say that only the father or both the father and the bridegroom are the ones who choose the bride, not the reverse.

Concerning that, Rabbi Simon says: [Why did the Torah say: *"If any man takes a wife..." (Deut. 22:13)* and didn't say *"If any woman takes a husband"?* Because that's the tradition, that the man goes to find the woman, the woman does not go to find the man. You can compare that to a man who lost something. Who goes to find the other? The one who lost the object is the one who goes to search for it. Therefore, the man who lost one of his ribs (when God took a rib from Adam to create Eve) is the one who seeks to restore it].[65]

A verse from the New Testament raises our level of understanding of this step of marriage: *"You did not choose Me, but I chose you and appointed you that you should go and bear fruit, and that your fruit should remain..." (John 15:16).* We see clearly here that God the Father chooses the church as a bride in the name of His

---

63 Shadkhan: This service was practically indispensable in ancient times and was used by many Jewish families who lived in a conservative and strict community. It involved collecting and evaluating information about the personal characteristics and economic, social and cultural background of the prospective spouses in order to ensure a happy and holy marriage. The fee for the matchmaker performing this service was, as usual, a percentage of the dowry. It is worth noting that this service is now carried out by many websites and digital applications in what is known as Online dating applications.

64 Encyclopædia Britannica, Shadkhan.

65 Goldwurm, Hersh, Nosson Scherman, Yisroel S. Schorr, and Chaim Malinowitz. Talmud Bavli: [talmud Bavli] : The Schottenstein Edition : the Gemara : the Classic Vilna Edition, with an Annotated, Interpretive Elucidation, As an Aid to Talmud Study. , 1990. Print. Kiddushin 2b2.

son. And the Son loved her even before she loved Him as he trusts that His father's choices are the best. So *"We love Him because He first loved us." (1 John 4:19).*

2. As for the bride, she did not get to see her Bridegroom to-be most of the time[66]. Nevertheless, she knew more about him from the messenger servant sent by the father in his son's name to betroth her. As with the church, the messengers' role here symbolizes the work of the Holy Spirit[67]. Perhaps the contemporary church has not witnessed the Son in His days of incarnation on earth, but she knew about him through the Holy Spirit sent from the Father in the Name of the Son to teach her everything about the Bridegroom[68]. Therefore, apostle Peter says about Christ the Bridegroom: *"whom having not seen you love. Though now you do not see Him, yet believing, you rejoice with joy inexpressible and full of glory" (1 Peter 1:8)* The holy spirit allows the Church, the bride, to see Jesus the Bridegroom with eyes of faith. This is the Holy Spirit working in the sacrament of the Eucharist allowing us to see the Bridegroom every day on the altar[69].

The Holy Spirit brings to the Son new brides every day! Human souls, believing in Him and experiencing Him as a Bridegroom. We are witnesses to the work of the Holy Spirit in repentance and evangelism as mentioned in *"...no one can say that Jesus is Lord[70] except by the Holy Spirit." (1 Co 12:3).*

---

66 Mendell Lewittes: Jewish Marriage, Rabbinic Law, Legend, and Custom, Jason Aronson Inc., 1994, P 41.

67 Note: the name of Eliezer means help/assistance.

68 "But the Helper, the Holy Spirit, whom the Father will send in My name, **He will teach you all things,** and bring to your remembrance all things that I said to you." (John 14:26).

69 **We behold You upon the altar every day and we partake of your Body and Your precious Blood,** from the Coptic Hymns "Pi-Oik" chanted during the distribution of the communion according to the rite of the Divine Liturgy in the Coptic Orthodox Church.

70 From the Greek κύριος, means Lord.

Christ Betroths the Bride

We should not forget that the Holy Spirit, the Lord the Giver of Life, is the One who spoke by the prophets in the Old Testament and made them betrothIsrael, the bride, to "Jehovah" the Bridegroom. He also spoke by the apostles in the New Testament and made them spiritual matchmakers for Christ the Bridegroom. That is why our teacher, the apostle Paul, said to the Corinthians: *"For I am jealous for you with godly jealousy. For I have betrothed you to one husband, that I may present you as a chaste virgin to Christ."* (2 Co 11:2).

3. We read in the Parable of the Wedding Feast in Matt. 22 about a king-father who made a wedding feast for his son and chose the invitees, yet the wedding was burdensome to them, so "they were not willing to come" (Verse 3). They were not invited to participate from afar as audiences or as mere friends, but they were chosen as a bride to the son, the Bridegroom, on an eternal plane. This invitation was to enter into an everlasting joy without interruption. However, the soul, the bride, because of her inner misery rejects the joy and lives in sorrow which does not originate from external conditions, but from a closed heart which refuses to open up to Christ the Bridegroom, the giver of joy and peace. Those invitees symbolize those who reject the work of the Holy Spirit to sanctify the soul as a bride to Jesus Christ.

In his commentary on this parable, Reverend Father Tadros Yacoub Malaty says: [What is this Heavenly Kingdom except for the church whose reality is a continuous wedding, as the Father established her for His Son to enjoy her, and she enjoys His presence in her midst, and by leaning against His chest, she accepts from Him His Father's secrets and rejoices with His divine abilities, until she is lifted up with Him and in Him to His Father's bosom, sharing His Glory][71].

---

[71] Father Tadros Yacoub Malati: A Series of Interpretation and reflections of the Early

Prayer: Why would the King of kings and the Lord of lords choose my weary soul to be His bride? I don't deserve it. Behold me saying with the Song of Song's bride: *"I am the rose of Sharon⁷², And the lily of the valleys."*. I'm just an ordinary flower with no special beauty. But my Bridegroom answers my soul: *"Like a lily among thorns, so is my love among the daughters."* So, let me ornament myself with repentance and not reject the work of His Holy Spirit. Let me stop my spiritual adultery and my attachment to anything else except my love to my Bridegroom. Let me ask the Spirit to speak to me about Him and His beauty…to acquaint me with Him more and more... to love Him as He loved me first.

Step 2: Paying the Dowry

Before proceeding to explain this step of marriage, I would like to clarify that the details which will be mentioned here pertain to the Jewish traditions in marriage. It might not be consistent with the culture of equality between man and woman in which we live in the modern world, established by Christianity as mentioned for example in *1 Co 11:11 "Nevertheless, neither is man independent of woman, nor woman independent of man, in the Lord."*, also in Gal 3:28 *"There is neither Jew nor Greek, there is neither slave nor free, there is neither male nor female; for you are all one in Christ Jesus."* However, for the sake of portraying reality, the way women were treated in ancient Israel is considered much more refined in comparison with treatment of women in pagan (gentile) nations. There was no worth at all for women, nor for marriage, which was fulfilled once any man took home any woman he wanted to sleep with, thus becoming his wife. God in the Old Testament establishes important principles in marriage like holiness and continuity. Consequently, the dowry was meant as an appreciation to the

---

Fathers / Gospel of Matthew- Chapter 22.

72 Sharon: שָׁרוֹן is a Hebrew word, means normal.

woman, raising her from merely a being to satisfy man's lust to a valuable human with rights.

Concerning that, Rabbi Morris Lam says: [Before the revelation in Sinai, a man would meet any woman on the road, and if he wanted to marry her, he would take her to his house and have sex with her without witnesses or publicity. However, when the Torah[73] was given, the instructions were clear to the Jews that when they wanted to take a wife, a man would not marry her except in the presence of witnesses, then she would become his wife. After her engagement, even if she is sleeping with the man or living with him in his house, she is considered his wife. And any other man who tries to take her is considered guilty and deserves punishment and vengeance. If he wants to leave her, he must divorce her first].[74]

After this necessary introduction, let us speak about the second step, following the choosing of the bride comes the paying of the dowry.

1. In ancient Israel, the bride was bought with a price. This price was paid for two main reasons:

b. To compensate the father for losing a laborer of his family. In an agricultural shepherding society like ancient Israel, women used to work like men. In marriage, the father loses a working hand which contributes to earning profit, helps with living expenses, and raises the rest of the children.

---

[73] Torah: In Hebrew הָרוֹת means law, teaching, or guidance. It usually means the Pentateuch, meaning Genesis, Exodus, Leviticus, Number and Deuteronomy. It is five out of the 24 books that make up the Tanakh (the Jewish Bible) and it is usually printed with the interpretations of Jewish rabbis known as the Perushim so it contains all from the written law בתכבש הרות and the Oral Tradition הרות. Sometimes the word Torah is used to mean all the books of the Tanakh from Genesis to Malachi. At other times, it refers to all Jewish teachings, legislation and practices, whether they appeared in the Tanakh or in the writings of rabbis throughout the ages.

[74] Rabbi Maurice Lamm: The Jewish Way in Love & Marriage, Jonathan David Publishers, inc, 2008, P 10.

c. To compensate the father for what he spent on raising this bride including providing shelter, clothing, food, etc.

In Deuteronomy 24:1 it says: *"When a man takes a wife and marries her..."*. The word "takes" used here is the Hebrew word "חָקַל - lâqach" and it's used for trading in selling and buying.[75]

Women in such early times of human history were considered property, the Hebrew word for wife הָלְעַב - Ba'ălâh directly translates to "property" and the Hebrew word for husband לַעַב - ba'al directly translates to "owner". In Ex 20:17, woman is put in the same list along with other possessions as it says: *"You shall not covet your neighbor's house; you shall not covet your neighbor's wife, nor his male servant, nor his female servant, nor his ox, nor his donkey, nor anything that is your neighbor's."*

2. However, we can conclude that the dowry paid to the bride's father was compensation more so than a price for buying and selling. It was considered an appreciation for the value of the bride, for whenever the more precious the dowry, the more deserving the bride. For example, the dowry of virgins was twice the price of the widowed and the divorced[76]. The bridegroom could pay more if he wanted, and the more he paid, the more he loved his bride. For example, if the specified dowry for the bride was 3 camels, 50 shekels[77] of silver, a tent, or other, the bridegroom was free to pay more as an appreciation of his bride.

3. The dowry was not always money, jewels or gold, but we see a disparity in the value of the dowry according to the

---

75 Mendell Lewittes: Jewish Marriage, Rabbinic Law, Legend, and Custom, Jason Aronson Inc., 1994, P 67.

76 Philip and Hanna Goodman: The Jewish Marriage anthology, The Jewish Publication Society of America, 1971, P 70,89.

77 Caliber name for weighing valuables and more.

circumstances of the marriage, the economic, and social status of both parties. Here are some examples from the Bible:

a. Isaac offers gold jewelry to Rebecca in (Genesis 24:22) *"...a golden nose ring weighing half a shekel, and two bracelets for her wrists weighing ten shekels of gold."* The nose ring was to be worn in the nose or the ear, the bracelet was worn on the forearm or above the elbow, and it was made in the form of chains, tapes, or sheets. These certainly were precious gifts as nothing was more valuable than gold at that time.

b. Jacob offered years of his life as a dowry to Rachel as per Gen 29:20 *"So Jacob served seven years for Rachel, and they seemed only a few days to him because of the love he had for her."* However, he was deceived and given "Leah," so he had to serve another seven years to take Rachel as ordered by his uncle Laban (Gen 29:27) *"...and we will give you this one also for the service which you will serve with me still another seven years."* Years of one's life are undoubtedly more precious than gold. It is worth mentioning that Jacob lived 147 years. This means that the dowry he offered to his wife "Rachel" reached about 10% of his life in years. Truly the dowry paid by "Jacob" was more precious than the one paid by his father "Isaac" to his mother "Rebecca".

c. David paid a more precious and even more unusual dowry! We read about this strange dowry in 1 Sam 18:20-28 when "Saul" asked his servants cunningly to talk to "David" about his marriage to Mikal his daughter, and when "David" felt his inability to offer a proper dowry to the king's daughter, the answer came to him that the king does not delight in the dowry but in victory over his enemies, asking for 100 foreskins of the Philistines. Saul's purpose was to kill David.

However, "David" and his men killed 200 men and came to Saul with 200 foreskins[78] before the predetermined time and married "Mikal" who loved him. We see that "David" did not offer years of his life, but he put his life on the line as a dowry for his bride, the king's daughter. Truly the dowry paid by David was more precious than those paid by "Isaac" and "Jacob".

d. But If Jesus Christ is the Bridegroom, what is the dowry he paid for the church, his bride?

- We describe the church in the Divine Liturgy saying: "This which You have acquired to Yourself with the **Precious blood** of Your Christ".[79]

- Christ the Bridegroom truly offered the most precious dowry that could ever be paid! He gave His life on the cross. Our teacher saint Paul says: *"Just as Christ also loved the church and gave Himself for her"* (Ephesians 5:25). This dowry was paid by the Bridegroom, the incarnated Son, according to His Father's will and out of His abundant love to the church as the bible says: *"For God so loved the world that He gave His only begotten Son, that whoever believes in Him should not perish but have everlasting life."* (John 3:16)

- In this manner, the cross became the dowry. It became proof of love and appreciation for the bride, the church. As the bride is proud of her dowry, the church is proud of the cross. But she considers this dowry the only reason for her pride[80], that is why the apostle Paul says: *"But God forbid that I*

---

78 The foreskin: is the piece of skin that is cut off at circumcision.

79 From the prayers of the litanies in the Divine Liturgy of Saint Basil the Great, according to the rite of the Coptic Orthodox Church.

80 The Coptic Church celebrates the Cross on the 17th of Tut and the 10th of Baramhat every year. It is also celebrated by the Western Churches on the 3rd of May.

should boast except in the cross of our Lord Jesus Christ..." (Gal 6:14).

- As the bridegroom's father rejoices when his son offers the dowry to his beloved bride, likewise the Father rejoices with what the Son has done as per Isaiah 53:10: *"Yet it pleased the Lord to bruise Him...".* In fact,, the Son Himself, on account of His great love to His bride, set His own joy before Him as He offered the dowry, so He endured the pain joyfully as mentioned in Hebrews 12:2: *"...who for the joy that was set before Him endured the cross, despising the shame...".* Thus, the cross became a sign of joy! As it is a sign of the Bridegroom's strength in enduring pain for the sake of His bride, as Saint Paul said "For the message of the cross is foolishness to those who are perishing, but to us who are being saved it is the power of God." (1 Co 1:18). It is the Bridegroom's cross which showed with weakness that which is greater than power[81].

- The New Testament mentioned this dowry many times, as it is not just silver or gold *"knowing that you were not redeemed with corruptible things, like silver or gold, from your aimless conduct received by tradition from your fathers, but with the precious blood of Christ, as of a lamb without blemish and without spot." (1 Peter 1:18-19).* The dowry was also referred to as a guarantee in the Bible as mentioned in *Ephesians 1:14: "who is the guarantee of our inheritance until the redemption of the purchased possession, to the praise of His glory."* Jesus Christ clearly mentions the price of His church in the last supper, right before He pays it all, as mentioned in Luke 22:19: *"And He took bread, gave thanks*

---

81 By weakness showed forth what it is greater than power: from the Coptic Hymns "Omonogenes", "O, only-begotten Son", chanted in the sixth hour of the Good Friday, in the ordination of the patriarchs and bishops and in the consecration of the Chrism (holy anointing oil– Myron) according to the rite of the Coptic Orthodox Church.

and broke it, and gave it to them, saying, "This is My body which is given for you; do this in remembrance of Me." Regarding the church, the bible says that God purchased her with His own blood, that is why there is a warning to the leaders and pastors, *"Therefore take heed to yourselves and to all the flock, among which the Holy Spirit has made you overseers, to shepherd the church of God which, He purchased with His own blood." (Acts 20:28).*

4. According to Jewish traditions, the payment of the dowry occurs in the bride's house. Jesus Christ also paid the price on earth. Accordingly, His birth in the fullness of time was inevitable as it was necessary to pay the dowry of His expatriate bride on earth. Since the dowry should be handed to the bride's father, Jesus the Bridegroom surrendered His spirit in the hands of the Father of the church (The Heavenly Father), therefore He said: *"...Father, 'into Your hands I commit My spirit." (Luke 23:46)* as though He was saying to the father, here I deliver to you the dowry of my bride, the church, who calls you her dad[82].

5. As the bride was bought with a price, she belongs to her Bridegroom. Similarily, we do not belong to ourselves, but we belong to Christ the Bridegroom who paid the price which is His life on the cross. We see this in 1 Co 7:23 as the Bible warns us about being governed by anyone but the Bridegroom, saying: *"You were bought at a price; do not become slaves of men."* And in 1 Co 6:19,20, our teacher Saint Paul says that our bodies and spirits are not ours, but they are for the Bridegroom Who paid their price in full: *"Or do you not know that your body is the temple of the Holy Spirit who is in you, whom you have from God, and you are not*

---

[82] Revise "So He said to them, "When you pray, say: Our Father in heaven, Hallowed be Your name. Your kingdom come. Your will be done On earth as it is in heaven. (Luke 11:2).

your own? For you were bought at a price; therefore, glorify God in your body and in your spirit, which are God's." and in Luke 22:19-20. Saint Paul the apostle also says: *"Oh, that you would bear with me in a little folly—and indeed you do bear with me." (2 Co 11:1).*

6. In Jeremiah 31:22, the Bible says, *"...For the Lord has created a new thing in the earth—A woman shall encompass a man."* As an nod to a newfound Jewish custom pertaining to marriage, a ceremony called "The Seven Circuits[83]" in which the bridegroom stands in the middle and the bride spins around him seven times as a sign of her submission, love, and belonging to him. This ceremony is practiced in Jewish marriages[84] today. Here, we clearly see Christ the Bridegroom in the center and the church declaring her love and belonging to Him through her Seven Sacraments. Additionally, in the Bible, to surround symbolizes protection as mentioned in Deut. 32:10: *"...He encircled him, He instructed him, He kept him as the apple of His eye."* The church, the bride, is entrusted with the Bridegroom's seven sacraments, as she is the one who practices them with seriousness and integrity[85].

7. When Jesus Christ surrendered His life on the cross *"...He said: It is finished..." (John 19:30).* The word "finished" in the Greek origin is τελέω - teleō which means "finished" or

---

[83] Some Jews interpret it as a reminder of the seven days of creation as the newlyweds create their own world in marriage. While some see it as a reminder of the seven great shepherds of Israel; Abraham, Isaac, Jacob, Moses, Aaron, Joseph and David so the newlyweds ask for their blessings. Also, some of the interpreters say that it is a reminder of the seven cycles around the walls of Jericho mentioned in (Josh 6:15), in the desire of the newlyweds to demolish any walls or barriers between them.

[84] Targum Pess: The Eternal Bond / A Guide to the Laws, Customs & Traditions of the Jewish Wedding, Chaim Press, 2008, P 110 – 111.

[85] This is what we sing in the Coptic song "Arous al-Fadi" (a song from the Coptic heritage). We say to the church: "Oh, my mother, how faithful you were, and with the love of your Bridegroom, you are fascinated, His myteries are hidden with you, and by His strength you are protected."

"completed[86]." It is this very word which is used to express "to pay the price" or "to settle a debt" in the Bible[87]. Could it be that the last words Jesus said on the cross were about His bride? Was His bride the last thing He was thinking about before He delivered His life? Why not?! His bride has always been in His heart, so would she not also be on his lips?!

Prayer: My heavenly King...I say with the apostle John *"Greater love has no one than this, than to lay down one's life for his friends" (John 15:13)* But, do I deserve all this love? My King, You paid the greatest dowry anyone could ever pay. You Have paid neither silver nor gold, but You paid Your life as a price and bought me with Your precious blood...I am not mine anymore, then, but yours! I give you my body, soul, desires, emotions, feelings, dreams, and ambitions. I give you everything. I give you my whole life to be totally unto you, with you and for you.

Step 3: The Covenant and Ketuba

1. In the engagement ritual, the bridegroom's father presents the marriage contract[88] to the bride's father, which is named "הָבוּתְּכ Ketubah" which means "that which is written." It was a written commitment, mentioning the value of the dowry and the bridegroom's other commitments towards his bride[89]. Before the ketubah, women were devoid of rights: no safety, no guarantee of protection or commitment. The ketubah was

---

86 James Strong: S.T.D.,LL.D., A Concise Dictionaryof the word in the Greek Testament, Abingdon Press, 1890, P 71.

87 Revise "When they had come to Capernaum, those who received the temple tax came to Peter and said, "Does your Teacher not pay (τελέω) the temple tax?" (Matthew 17:24), And also "For because of this you also pay taxes, for they are God's ministers attending continually to this very thing." (Romans 13:6).

88 There are some other cultures that took the marriage contract from the Jews and called it " writing the marriage contract ", and it may be connected or separated from them on the wedding day (popularly known as the Dokhla), just like the Jewish tradition.

89 Barney Kadsan: God's Appointed Customs/ A Messianic Jewish Guide to the Biblical Lifecycle and Lifestyle, Messianic Jewish Publishers, 1996, P 49.

a legal document that gave value to women's rights in Jewish society.

2. In the ketubah, the bridegroom vows to the bride, in writing, to support her, love her, be faithful to her, protect her, provide for her, and to live with her forever and never leave her. The ketubah as a document is specially designed to be a wonderful piece of art in terms of the drawings and colors as the bride loves to keep it all her life and makes sure to display it in her home. The ketubah still holds a special place among Jewish marriage rituals even to this day, regardless of their denomination[90]. The ketubah is read aloud to the invitees over several instances and the bride is usually pleased with her ketubah for what it holds from meanings and vows.

3. The Holy Bible is the ketubah given by the Bridegroom to his bride, as it holds God's promises for us. It truly includes all the promises mentioned in the ketubah in the Jewish marriage ritual.

Some view the Bible as a book forbidding many things, but this is not the case at all. It is a marriage contract that shows us the gifts we are given as a bride to Jesus. For all the biblical promises are considered vows that we believe will happen, they are a love letter between the Bridegroom and his bride, the church. For example, Christ the Bridegroom vows in a writing in Matt. 6:28-30: *"So why do you worry about clothing? Consider the lilies of the field, how they grow: they neither toil nor spin; and yet I say to you that even Solomon in all his glory was not arrayed like one of these. Now if God so clothes the grass of the field, which today is, and tomorrow is thrown into the oven, will He not much more clothe you, O you of little faith?"* Here, our heavenly Bridegroom promises that he will feed us, clothe us, and provide for all our needs. He is in a covenant with us and our ketubah is a witness to that.

---

[90] There are many changes that have taken place in the Jewish marriage rituals. Orthodox and conservative Jews, for example, use a different formula than other Jewish sects.

4. The ketubah was given first to Israel (in the Old Testament) but it was given afterward to every human, meaning that the non-Jews who were outside the area of God's covenant before are now entering God's covenant and can now enjoy the bride's blessings.

The truth is that in the church the bride has gained promises that are much more beautiful than those acquired by Israe,l as the apostle Paul said: ***"But now He has obtained a more excellent ministry, inasmuch as He is also Mediator of a better covenant, which was established on better promises." (Hebrews 8:6)***

5. In this newer and greater covenant, our heavenly Bridegroom vows to change the concept of the ketubah by taking the external code and putting it in our hearts. He will transform it from being a mere collection of laws and legislations to an intrinsic lived experience for us to live by to deepen our knowledge of Him. Thus the Christian becomes a living gospel. We may find one in a hundred reading the Bible, but the other ninety-nine read the Christian himself! We read in Jeremiah:

"Behold, the days are coming, says the Lord, when I will make a new covenant with the house of Israel and with the house of Judah— not according to the covenant that I made with their fathers in the day that I took them by the hand to lead them out of the land of Egypt, My covenant which they broke, though I was a husband to them, says the Lord. But this is the covenant that I will make with the house of Israel after those days, says the Lord: I will put My law in their minds, and write it on their hearts; and I will be their God, and they shall be My people. No more shall every man teach his neighbor, and every man his brother, saying, 'Know the Lord,' for they all shall know Me, from the least of them to the greatest of them, says the Lord. For I will

forgive their iniquity, and their sin I will remember no more."
(Jeremiah 31:31-34)

Prayer: My heavenly prince…I am now Holy to you…my soul is sanctified and holy to you alone…and as the bride consecrates her ketubah I concentrate mine as well. Your holy words are a spiritual harp, where Your Holy Spirit plays the greatest symphony of love. I will not hang it on the wall, but I will keep it in my heart to examine you and know you more as my loving Bridegroom. I trust in your vows. Grant me faithfulness in my vows for here I say with prophet David: *"Accept, I pray, the freewill offerings of my mouth, O Lord." (Psalm 118:108)*[91]

Step 4: The Bride's Approval

1. Though the bride is chosen by the Bridegroom's father and is not the one who chooses her Bridegroom, she still has the final say and the upper hand in approving or rejecting the offer of marriage and we see that in the Rebecca's engagement in Gen. 24:57-58 after meeting "Eliezer the Damascus," Abraham's servant, at the well where she brought him to her father's house where the marriage offer was discussed between the bride Rebecca and the bridegroom Isaac, the son of Abraham. The next morning: "So they said, we will call the young woman and ask her personally. Then they called Rebekah and said to her, will you go with this man? And she said, I will go." and Rebecca gave her approval.

2. Marriage in Judaism is only achieved when both parties are in agreement. This was in the days when underage marriage was normative. This is why the rabbis said: "The man is forbidden from marrying his underage daughter until she is

---

[91] About the Septuagint translation of the Psalm written in the Book of Prayers of the Coptic Agpeya, which is Psalm 119 in the translation of Smith and Van Dyck (Psalm 119: 108) "Accept, I pray, the freewill offerings of my mouth, O Lord, And teach me Your judgments..".

an adult and can say that I choose this man"[92].

3. This also happens to us as brides of Jesus. God does not at all coerce anyone into agreeing to be a bride for his Son Jesus. He created us with free will. Certainly, He rejoices when we reciprocate his Son with the love which is generously outpoured on us, but he does not oblige us to do so. It was said in ancient times "among the terms of the relationship is the approval".

4. How does everyone know that the bride has accepted the marriage? The bride agrees to the marriage contract, the "ketubah" and shows her approval in a practical way. The human soul which God calls to be His bride should believe in Jesus, the Bridegroom, and should also take on the role of the bride. What benefit is there to accepting the marriage covenant (faith) without acting accordingly (with actions)? This is why the apostle Saint James says: "Thus also faith by itself, if it does not have works, is dead." (James 2:17). Rebecca agreed to marry Isaac whom she did not see (faith) but she left her father's house and went (actions) with "Eliezer the Damascus", truly her faith was practical[93].

5. What happens if the bride forgets her covenant and drifts away from her bridegroom? If the bride transgresses the covenant's conditions, she must return and look in her ketubah to remind herself that she accepted all its conditions

---

[92] Goldwurm, Hersh, Nosson Scherman, Yisroel S. Schorr, and Chaim Malinowitz. Talmud Bavli: [talmud Bavli] : the Schottenstein Edition : the Gemara : the Classic Vilna Edition, with an Annotated, Interpretive Elucidation, As an Aid to Talmud Study. , 1990. Print. Kiddushin 41a.

[93] The company of the bride symbolizes the Church of Christ the Bridegroom. Rebekah was beautiful and good looking, and the church was beautiful with its rituals, prayers and spirituality. It was a generous company, as it gave Eliezer of Damascus water and watered his ten camels (one camel may drink 200 liters of water if it is thirsty), and the church offers secrets and prayers to all believers throughout the days to quench their thirsty souls. Rebekah was a virgin whom no man knew, and the Church is also faithful and keeps her purity because of her strong love for her Bridegroom.

willingly and that she should get back to him. Repentance, then, is a return to respecting the conditions which the bride willingly assumed the day she accepted to remain with the Bridegroom for the rest of her life. It is as though the bride returns to her wedding day and as she cries tears of joy, so the soul cries to her heavenly Bridegroom as she returns to Him in the sacrament of repentance and confession. As for her Bridegroom, He cannot stand to see the tears in her eyes, so He tells her: *"Turn your eyes away from me, For they have overcome me."* *(Song of Songs 6:5)*

Prayer: My Good God…You gave me the freedom of choice and I chose you and accepted you to be my heavenly Bridegroom. Grant me to fulfill the promises of my covenant. Grant me to walk always with you and if I deviate, teach me to repent[94] and give me springs of tears as you once gave this sinful lady. Grant me to always remember the day I accepted you to be my Bridegroom, the day I believed in all your promises. Give that faith which operates with love[95], the genuine faith which testifies that You are my one and only Bridegroom so that I may grow in Your knowledge. Knowing you burns my heart with a desire to know you even better.

Step 5: The Covenant's Cup

After the bride accepts the ketubah conditions, the newlyweds drink a cup of wine to seal the marriage covenant. It is nice to know that the Hebrew word for "bridegroom" is circumcision[96] "חָתָן", which means the one who enters a covenant.

---

[94] From the conclusion of the Adam Theotokos (Your mercies, my God) "And I am also a sinner, my lord, teach me, to make repentance." From the midnight prayer, according to the rite of the Coptic Orthodox Church.

[95] Look at "For in Christ Jesus neither circumcision nor uncircumcision avails anything, but faith working through love." (Galatians 5:6).

[96] Joyce Elsenberg & Ellen Scolnic: Dictionary of Jewish Words, The Jewish Publication Society, 2001, P 61.

1. Actually, wine has been considered blessed for thousands of years, to such an extent that no covenant was made without drinking a cup of wine and saying "Blessed are you Lord king of the universe who creates the fruit of the vine". The newlyweds then share in one cup as a symbol of sharing in their upcoming life together.

2. We should understand that wine in Judaism symbolizes two important objects, which are:

a. Joy, as it says in the psalm: *"And wine that makes glad the heart of man, Oil to make his face shine" (Psalm 104:5).* In the Jewish understanding, marriage is the highest form of earthly joy. According to the Talmud, the unmarried person is without happiness, blessings, protection or peace[97].

b. Blood on account of its red color. Sharing in the same cup symbolizes the blood becoming one as the two become one body[98] in one life, in an everlasting bond.

3. As for this cup which Jesus gives to his church to drink with him, it resembles the following:

a. **Eucharistic Cup**[99]: the cup given by Jesus the Bridegroom in the last supper is the cup of a **new covenant** with His bride the church, as He said these divine words: *"...This cup is the new covenant in My blood, which is shed for you." (Luke 22:20)*

b. **Cup of Pain**: from what we understand from the conversation between Jesus and the mother of Zebedee's sons, drinking

---

[97] Ari L. Goldman: Being Jewish, The Spiritual and Cultural Practice of Judaism Today, Simon & Schuster Paperback, 2000, P 70.

[98] Look at "Therefore a man shall leave his father and mother and be[k] joined to his wife, and they shall become one flesh" (Genesis 2:24).

[99] Eucharist: its origin is a Greek word ἡ εὐχαριστία, which means thanksgiving, and it is called the sacrament of communion.

from the cup is a symbol for the enduring of pain as we read in Matthew 20:20-23: *"Then the mother of Zebedee's sons came to Him with her sons, kneeling down and asking something from Him. And He said to her, "What do you wish?" She said to Him, "Grant that these two sons of mine may sit, one on Your right hand and the other on the left, in Your kingdom. But Jesus answered and said, "You do not know what you ask. Are you able to drink the cup that I am about to drink, and be baptized with the baptism that I am baptized with?" They said to Him, We are able. So He said to them, "You will indeed drink My cup, and be baptized with the baptism that I am baptized with; but to sit on My right hand and on My left is not Mine to give, but it is for those for whom it is prepared by My Father."* This is why Jesus said to Peter when he cut the ear of the high priest's servant: *"So Jesus said to Peter, "Put your sword into the sheath. Shall I not drink the cup which My Father has given Me?" (John 18:11)*. Similarly, Jesus the Bridegroom prayed to his heavenly father in Gethsemane saying: *"Abba, Father, all things are possible for You. Take this cup away from Me; nevertheless, not what I will, but what You will." (Mark 14:36)*

4. When we look at the last supper through the Jewish disciples' perspective, we see that they were celebrating the Passover, the commemoration of God's marriage covenant with Israel in Exodus. It is as though Jesus the Bridegroom was saying to them that God who gave the old covenant in Sinai is the same One who is giving the new covenant right now. And because this covenant is new, both the church, the bride, and her Bridegroom should drink from the same cup (whether a cup of pain or joy) so she may live with Him through crucifixion and resurrection.

5. There is another cup the newlyweds will drink from months later, when the bridegroom takes his bride to live together in their home and this is what Jesus meant when He said: ***"But I say to you, I will not drink of this fruit of the vine from now on until that day when I drink it new with you in My Father's kingdom." (Matthew 26:29)***

6. Since the cup of the covenant in this step which seals the marriage covenant resembles the Eucharist, it means that every time we take communion, we should remember His covenants as a Bridegroom and our vows as a bride. For this reason, in every liturgy, we read the Bible (his covenant) and we pray for our repentance and purity (our vows).

Prayer: My God and Lord… I thank You for not having shut me out, I the sinful one, but You called me even though I do not deserve to drink from Your precious blood, so Lord, lover of mankind, who died for us, resurrected, and gave us Your living sacraments, to sanctify our bodies and souls, grant them to be mine as well, to heal my body and soul, to enlighten my heart. I will drink this cup with You…I welcome pain as long as it is for You…I will go through it with You and I will rejoice with You in victory as I am fully trusting that every Golgotha is followed by an empty tomb, and every cross ends with resurrection.

Step 6: The Bridegroom's Gifts to the Bride

1. Besides the Dowry, the bride also used to receive gifts from her Bridegroom. We read in Gen 24:53 about "Eliezer the Damascus" and how he "…brought out jewelry of silver, jewelry of gold, and clothing, and gave them to Rebekah. He also gave precious things to her brother and to her mother." No wonder as "the servant took ten of his master's camels and departed, for all his master's goods were in his hand" (Gen 24:10).

Rebekah had no idea that the camels she gave water to drink were camels carrying gifts for her, she did not even know that one of these camels would take her to her bridegroom, Isaac.

2. Gifts were of great importance to the bride, as they helped her to remember her bridegroom while he was away from her. With the evolution of marriage traditions, this gift became the ring (wedding band). Giving the bride a ring became a central part in the wedding ceremony. When the Jewish bridegroom puts the ring on the bride's finger (the fourth finger, known as the index finger) he used to say "By this ring, be Holy to me, according to the law of Moses and Israel"[100].

3. Similarly, the Holy Spirit becomes the wedding band which reminds the church of her Bridegroom. The Holy Spirit is the greatest gift to ever be given. This is precisely what Jesus Christ said to His bride, the church: ***"But the Helper, the Holy Spirit, whom the Father will send in My name, He will teach you all things, and bring to your remembrance all things that I said to you." (John 14:26)***. Thus, the apostle Saint Paul says in his second letter to the Corinthians: ***"Now He who establishes us with you in Christ and has anointed us is God, who also has sealed us and given us the Spirit in our hearts as a guarantee." (2 Corinthians 1:21-22)***. Through the Holy spirit we receive many gifts: ***"for to one is given the word of wisdom through the Spirit, to another the word of knowledge through the same Spirit, to another faith by the same Spirit, to another gifts of healings by the same Spirit, to another the working of miracles, to another***

---

[100] Ari L. Goldman: Being Jewish, The Spiritual and Cultural Practice of Judaism Today, Simon & Schuster Paperback, 2000, P 77.

prophecy, to another discerning of spirits, to another different kinds of tongues, to another the interpretation of tongues. But one and the same Spirit works all these things, distributing to each one individually as He wills." (1 Corinthians 12:8-11).

4. Is it possible for the bride to tell her Bridegroom: "I do not want any gifts" or "Why have you brought this gift? You should not have brought it!" This is what we do when we reject the work of the Holy Spirit[101]! This way, not only do we reject the gift, but the giver as well who is the Giver of all good gifts[102].

5. What is remarkable in this gift is that it is a fruitful gift. As the bride beholds her wedding ring, she remembers her bridegroom, which gives her *"... love, joy, peace, longsuffering, kindness, goodness, faithfulness, gentleness, self-control." (Galatians 5:22,23)*

Out of the excessive abundance of these gifts, the bride cannot stand keeping them for herself, but she would tell everyone saying: "Behold, my bridegroom's gifts. Look how much he loves me!" This is the meaning of the church's evangelism around the world.

Prayer: My beloved God... You gave me the most precious gift, the Holy Spirit whom You sent to Your saintly disciples and holy apostles. Grant me not to take this great gift for granted. Let Him be fruitful within me, so that He can shine for all those around me. And you, O Holy spirit, sanctify my depths. For You are the one who gives me true repentance. You always renew my thoughts and give me life. Shine on me from the heavens with your light. Come

---

101 Look at: "Do not quench the Spirit." (1 Thessalonians 5:19).

102 Look at: "Every good gift and every perfect gift is from above, and comes down from the Father of lights, with whom there is no variation or shadow of turning." (James 1:17).

along the giver of life and enlighten my heart. Grant me comfort for my pain. Soften what has grown stiff within me and remove the heart of stone from within me and give me a heart of flesh. So that I may testify to my Bridegroom and serve everyone, whoever and wherever they may be.

Step 7: The Mikvah

A design of the mikvah- source of water - diving spot- stair steps

1. The Jewish bride in old Israel and even to this day, must experience the "Mikvah-הְוְקְמָ" as a fundamental step in the marriage ritual. The Hebrew word "Mikvah" means "The pond of living water" and it is used as a ritual for purification. This rite, in Hebrew, is called "Tevilah- הָלִיבְט" and consists of complete immersion of the body in a basin of Mikvah water three times to prepare the soul and body for marriage.

2. In the Old Testament, water was used to purify from defilement as mentioned in Levites 15:5-8, 10,11. The word used to describe this rite is מָתָא לְבָטוּ which means "immersion" or "dipping" and this is why the Mishnah says: [Every time the Torah mentions washing the body and cloth from defilement, it is not achieved unless the full body is immersed in the Mikvah[103]]. According to Jewish law (Halakha הָכָלָה)[104], two main conditions must be fulfilled in each of the three dives, which are:

---

103 Herbert Danby: The Code of Maimonides/Book 10/The Book of Cleanness/Treatise 8/ Immersion Pools, New Haven Yale University Press, 1954, P 497.

104 Jewish Law - הָכָלָה - Halakha: Halakhah in the Eastern word for it and Haluk in the Ashkenazi word, means Jewish law, which is the set of laws, traditions and religious guidelines that every Jew must follow. It contains 613 laws. The source of these laws are the biblical commandments, the teachings of the Talmud and the rabbinic teachings known as the Mitzvah (Hebrew: הָוְצַמ). It is worth noting that when debate rages among the Jewish clergy on any legal question, the discussion is called the halakhic debate, which usually ends with a result considered as a legal fatwa.

a. The entirety of the body must be immersed in water all at once. Meaning that each body part must not be immersed independently.

b. Nothing should separate the body from the water (such as clothing or anything else).

Jewish laws stipulate the importance of the ritual of the Mikvah since it cannot be postponed by the woman under any condition[105].

3. The Mikvah is a traditional Jewish ritual tinted with a deep symbolic dye in which we see God Himself purifying his people. He is the one who sanctifies them with purification laws. Concerning this, Rabbi Akiva says: [Blessed are you, O Israel, before whom are you purifying yourself? Who sanctifies you? Your Father who is in heaven... And as the Mikvah purifies uncleanness, so also is the Holy One, blessed is He, who cleanses Israel].

4. In light of everything previously stated, it becomes clear that the Mikvah is a symbol of baptism, which, to the church, the bride, is considered a holy sacrament and a primary condition for salvation. For this reason, in his conversation with Nicodemus, Jesus said: "Most assuredly, I say to you unless one is born of water and the Spirit, he cannot enter the kingdom of God" (John 3:5). He also said: "He who believes and is baptized will be saved, but he who does not believe will be condemned." (Mark 16:16).

5. Baptism, then, is not just for repentance for the forgiveness of sins (Mark 1:4) neither is it merely a divine order for the performance of a ritual before a major task (Matthew 28:19) nor is it just a step to join the church community (1 Co

---

[105] Rabbi Elyashiv Knohl: The Marriage Covenant / A Guide to Jewish Marriage, Leshon Limudim Ltd.,2008, P 89, 100.

12:13). However, because Jesus is the Bridegroom and the church is his bride, baptism is much more than just a sign of repentance or a religious ritual or an admission requirement, it is a shower taken before the wedding through which Jesus cleanses us from sin to be His bride! This is what Paul the apostle said: "Husbands, love your wives, just as Christ also loved the church and gave Himself for her, that He might sanctify and cleanse her with the washing of water by the word, that He might present her to Himself a glorious church, not having spot or wrinkle or any such thing, but that she should be holy and without blemish." (Ephesians 5:25-27)

6. Both the Mikvah and baptism happen through 3 dips. The similarity between the Mikvah and baptism was very clear to the first century Jews and Christians. The indication for this was what saint Cyril of Jerusalem[106] said in his ceremony to the catechumens: "When you hear scriptural texts about mysteries, you will have a spiritual awareness of things beyond your knowledge. If it were your wedding day, would you not have disregarded everything else and started preparing for the wedding day ceremony? And on the evening of the day you consecrate your soul to your heavenly Bridegroom, will you not give up the things of the flesh that you may win those of the spirit?"[107]

---

[106] St.Kerolos of Jerusalem: He was born in 315 AD and was ordained a deacon and then a priest. The bishop entrusted him with the task of teaching catechumens despite his young age, and made him preach on Sundays and holidays. Chosen Bishop of Jerusalem and he resisted the Arians, defending the correct education. He was exiled three times because of Arians' betrayals. but he's back to his throne and attended the Council of Constantinople and resisted Macedonius and Sabelius and other innovators, he departed in peace in the year 386 AD. His "articles for the catechumens" are considered Among his most important writings, which are twenty-four articles, eighteen of which were delivered approximately in 350 AD during the Lenten period, to those preparing for baptism in the Church of the Holy Sepulcher. These articles are of great importance as a witness to the rite of baptism and its theological concept in the fourth century AD.

[107] St. Cyril of Jerusalem / Procatechesis/ Prologue to the Catechetical Lectures of our Holy Father Cyril/ The Nicene and Post Nicene Fathers / Series2 / Volume 7 - Books for Ages/ AGES Software - Version 2.0, 1997 – Part 6 / P 110-111.

7. In the Jewish understanding, the Mikvah represents separation from an old life (the life of virginity) and the start of **a new life** (the bride's life). In Christianity, baptism is a symbol for the death of Jesus and his burial, thus it is the beginning of **a new life with Christ** the Bridegroom and concerning this, our teacher Paul the apostle says: "Therefore we were buried with Him through baptism into death, that just as Christ was raised from the dead by the glory of the Father, even so we also should walk in **newness[108] of life**." (Romans 6:4). In Judaism, the Mikvah represents a **change in authority**, for the woman is no longer under the authority of her father, but she is now the responsibility of her Bridegroom. Similarly, in Christianity, baptism also represents a **change in authority**, for Satan no longer has authority over the bride, and she has now become the responsibility of her Bridegroom, Jesus.

8. There was an old Christian tradition in the early church requiring those newly joining the church to take off their old clothes before baptism and wear new white clothes after baptism. In fact, it still happens in traditional churches whether for the baptism of children or adults. Concerning this, Saint Cyril of Jerusalem said in his ceremony to the catechumens: Directly after, before entering (into the baptismal water), you took off your clothes. This was a symbol of taking off the old man with his deeds (Colossians 3:9). And by taking off the clothes, you were naked, resembling Christ who was naked on the cross. The soul that has been torn off, that old soul, is not apt to be worn again. Rather, say with the bride of the book of the Song of Songs: 'I have taken off my robe; How can I put it on again? I have washed my feet; How can I defile them? (Song 5:3). And they were both naked, the man and

---

108 Newness: Greek καινότης - kainotēs, which is derived from καινός, meaning new. Look at: James Strong: S.T.D.,LL.D., A Concise Dictionary of the word in the Greek Testament, Abingdon Press, 1890, P 39.

his wife, and were not ashamed. (Genesis 2:25)][109]

9. The bride also used to be perfumed with fragrant oils after the "Mikvah". This is reminiscent of the myron oil[110] with which the baptized is oiled after the baptism.

10. In Matthew chapter 3, the Jews came to John the Baptist from Jerusalem, all of Judea, and all the region surrounding the Jordan river to be baptized and to repent from their sins. However, when John saw Jesus coming, he declared that they are not under his own responsibility (for he is but a friend of the Bridegroom), but that they are under the responsibility of the Bridegroom Himself, this is the reason for which he said: "Behold! The Lamb of God who takes away the sin of the world!" (John 1:29). John the Baptist wanted to clarify to the bride who her Bridegroom is, to surrender herself to Him.

11. Baptism also beautifully adorns the bride in her heavenly Bridegroom's eyes and of that, Saint Cyril of Jerusalem said to the catechumens: "The Lord will pour pure water on you, and you will be cleansed from all your sins. The angels of praise will surround you, singing: 'Who is this coming up from the wilderness, leaning upon her beloved? (Song 8:5). For the soul that was once a slave considers the Lord to be her relative, and He... will answer, saying: "Behold, you are fair, my love! Behold, you are fair!" (Song 4:1)]

---

[109] St. Cyril of Jerusalem / On The Mysteries of Baptism / Five Catechetical Lectures of our Holy Father Cyril/ The Nicene and Post Nicene Fathers / Series2 / Volume 7 - Books for Ages/ AGES Software - Version 2.0, 1997 - Lecture 20 / P 339.

[110] Myron: Chrism from the Greek Μύρον meaning "good oil." Or "fragrant oil", and it is called the sacrament of the holy anointing as it is called the same sacred oil with which anointing is practiced in this sacrament. The chrism is made from specific oils mixed with the spices that were offered at the shrouding of Christ.

St. Jacob Al-Srouji[111] says in his Maymar[112] about the holy baptism..." The braids of gold are for the bride who ascended from the water. Silver plates augment beauty for a lady of splendor. They bring sapphires from Chemosh to her high head, rows of precious stones from India, mountains present to you precious emeralds, and the depths send you pearls from their storehouses... Her Betrothed is rich; her beauty has many diverse forms...

The bride said: "rather than jewelry, to me, the cross is my adornment. Instead of braids of gold and coral, (the Bridegroom) shone on my face. Instead of silver plates, sanctify me. Instead of sapphires and rings, give me His nails, that I may make of them all the adornment of the engagement.]"[113]

Prayer: Bridegroom of my soul... Here I am, passed through the Mikvah, buried and risen again with You to live a new life, the life of a bride with her Bridegroom. I remember my heavenly birthday, the day I got baptized. Here I am, renewing my rejection of Satan and all his teaching and deceptions. And I declare my faith in the Holy Trinity, the one true God. Since I died with Christ and rose with him into a new life, I promise that I will no longer live for myself, but I will live for You alone for the rest of my life. Grant me, then, to take off my old man and put on the new one. As the bride leaves her father's house and becomes the responsibility of her Bridegroom, You too are now responsible for me and all my

---

111 St. Jacob Al-Srouji: He is considered a master of Syriac literature. He was born in Kartum on the bank of the Euphrates, which is one of the villages of Suruj, so he was nicknamed Al-Sarji. And his father was a priest. He obtained his theological education from the Persian School in Edessa and was a lover of purity and solitude since his childhood. His poetic and compositional talents appeared at the age of twenty. He was ordained bishop of the Diocese of Suruj in the year 519 AD. He was a contemporary of Anba Severus, Patriarch of Antioch. However, he did not remain in the bishopric for more than two years and then departed when he was seventy years old.

112 Maymar: a Syriac word meaning "to say." It is an essay or biography of a saint, and the plural is myamer. It is a poem that is read, not chanted, and it is an educational narrative.

113 Father Tadros Yacoub Malaty: A Daily Meeting with My God through the Experiences of the Fathers of the Early Church - Martyr George's Church, Pasporting - 2003 AD - p. 132.

needs. Therefore, if I need anything I will ask of You alone because in You, all my needs are fulfilled.

Step 8: The Bridegroom's departure

1. After having gone through all the previous steps and having written the marriage contract, the Jewish bridegroom takes a somewhat strange step, as he leaves his beloved bride to return to his father's house to prepare their marital home. The Jews use a Hebrew word "חָדַר - châdar" to describe this step, it means "curtain" and the word in it's Hebrew origin is a verb that means "embrace" or "enclose" as normally the marital home is a room adjoining the father's house[114]. This tradition is still present in some cultures and it is called "the family house" or "the big house" where the grandparent lives with their children and grandchildren.

2. The Torah established strict rules for marriage and according to these rules, the man has to build a house, plant a vineyard, and then proceed to marry a woman. This is what the wise Solomon declared in Proverbs: "Prepare your outside work, make it fit for yourself in the field; And afterward build your house." (Proverbs 24:27). Here, "prepare your outside work" means to prepare a place for living, "make it fit for yourself in the field" means to plant a vineyard, and "afterward build a house" means to marry a woman[115].

3. If the Jewish bridegroom is asked about his return date, he would say "Ask my father![116]" Indeed, as the return date

---

114 119 Barney Kadsan: God's Appointed Customs/ A Messianic Jewish Guide to the Biblical Lifecycle and Lifestyle, Messianic Jewish Publishers, 1996, P 60.

115 Goldwurm, Hersh, Nosson Scherman, Yisroel S. Schorr, and Chaim Malinowitz. Talmud Bavli: [talmud Bavli] : the Schottenstein Edition : the Gemara : the Classic Vilna Edition, with an Annotated, Interpretive Elucidation, As an Aid to Talmud Study. , 1990. Print. Sota 44a.

116 John Hagee: The Final Dawn Over Jerusalem, Thomas Nelson Inc., 1998, P 184.

Christ the Bridegroom

is dependent on the finishing of the place, and the place in question is in the father's house.

4. The bridegroom's absence may reach up to 12 months, but it never lasts less than nine months to confirm the virginity of the bride, her purity, and to ensure her lack of pregnancy[117]. During this period, the bride was tasked with preparing herself to leave her father's house and to live with her bridegroom's family, which reminds us of the psalm: "Listen, O daughter, Consider and incline your ear; **Forget your own people also, and your father's house**; So the King will greatly desire your beauty..." (Psalm 45:10-11).

5. Jesus spoke with His disciples about this step with complete honesty and He said: "In My Father's house are many mansions; if it were not so, I would have told you. **I go to prepare a place for you**. And if I go and prepare a place for you, **I will come again and receive you to Myself**; that where I am, there you may be also." (John 14:2,3). Because His father is the source of richness and all wealth[118] He has many mansions, enough for everyone. It should also be mentioned that the word for "mansions" is the Greek word μονή - monē which refer to "palaces" or "mansions"[119], proof of the wealth of the Bridegroom and His Father and also proof for His great love and appreciation of His bride who was well prepared His coming.

---

117 Ken Kessler: Understanding the Bride of Christ, Lifeschool International, 2010, P 19.

118 The original view of wealth in the Old Testament was that "Jehovah" As the Creator, he is the owner of everything because "the earth and its fullness belong to the Lord. the world and all those who dwell therein" (Psalm 24:1). In fact, the children of Israel were only agents on the land, and the Lord entrusted them to them according to the command of the Lord "and the land is not sold at all because the land is mine and you are strangers and mates with me" (Leviticus 25:23). See also (Numbers 33:53), (Deuteronomy 15:4) and (Deuteronomy 26:9). See the Christian Biblical Encyclopedia.

119 James Strong: S.T.D., LL.D., A Concise Dictionary of the word in the Greek Testament, Abingdon Press, 1890, P 49.

6. Our heavenly Bridegroom has left His bride and went to prepare a place for her and promised her to return to take her with Him. Although more than 2000 years have passed since He left, His promise still stands and His return is near. When He was asked about the time of His return, His answer was as the Jewish bridegroom's (ask my father) as He said: "But of that day and hour no one knows, not even the angels in heaven, nor the Son, **but only the Father**." (Mark 13:32). Certainly, Christ our Lord knows everything for it is said of Him: "in whom are hidden all the treasures of wisdom and **knowledge**" (Co 2:3). Here, He wanted to ensure that as a Bridegroom he would not reveal His return date. Saint Augustine[120] believed that Jesus Christ is not ignorant of the day, but He is revealing that he does not know it as intimately as the One who has control of the issue. Perhaps it is as when a teacher answers inquiries about his exams with "I do not know", meaning that he does not wish to reveal the questions[121].

7. When Jesus the Bridegroom wished to depart, he said to His bride that she would be better off if He left! Yes, He must depart to be return quickly[122]. However, He would not leave his bride without protection as He will the Holy Spirit to guide and comfort her. Therefore He said: "Nevertheless I

---

[120] Saint Augustine: He was born in 354 AD. The city of Tagest is one of the works of Numidia in North Africa. His mother "Monica" was a pious believer but his father Patrickpus was a rude pagan. Augustine grew up reckless in his life, prone to laziness. He went to Cartagena to learn the statement, and there he learned eloquence and the Latin language. However, he met wicked friends, became their leader, and turned his life into theaters and corruption. When she saw "Monica" That her son had perverted, her tears did not dry out, asking for his salvation. In Milan, he met Saint Ambrose, its bishop, who embraced him with his love and tenderness. Augustine loved him and admired his sermons, which were the reason for his repentance and changed his life. He was ordained a priest and then a bishop. So he repelled the heretics until he passed away peacefully in 430 AD. His works amounted to about 232 books. Among them are historical and polemical works against Jews, pagans, heretics, ascetic and moral works, as well as many biblical interpretations.

[121] Father Tadros Yacoub Malati: A Series of Interpretation and Meditations of the Early Fathers - Mark's Gospel - Chapter 13

[122] Refer to (Rev 22:7) "Behold, I am coming quickly..."

tell you the truth. **It is to your advantage that I go away;** for if I do not go away, the Helper will not come to you; but if I depart, I will send Him to you... However, when He, the Spirit of truth, has come, He will **guide you into all truth**; for He will not speak on His own authority, but whatever He hears He will speak; and He will tell you things to come. He will glorify Me, for He will take of what is Mine and declare it to you." (John 16:7, 13, 14).

Prayer: My Heavenly Prince... I know that You departed to prepare a home for me. I am sure that it is not an ordinary place, it is a mansion. What is more important to me is that I will be with You forever wherein resides never-ending joy. Wherein there will neither be subsequent departure nor separation. You promised to return to take me, and here I am, waiting for you, so do not slow down but come quickly.

Chapter 4

Christ Returns to Take the Bride

We discussed the steps of the first part of the traditional Jewish wedding in detail in the previous chapter "The Engagement", from choosing the bride until the bridegroom's departure and we saw Jesus the Bridegroom betrothing the Church to Himself. Now, we will discuss the second main part of the wedding which is the marriage.

The Bride's Waiting Period

1. The Jewish bride is now described as "כַּלָּה - kallâh" which means "spouse"[123], as she becomes as the wife who is paired with her husband, and she is holy and consecrated to him while he is preparing the place for her[124]. She used to be considered married, therefore she would be punished if she betrayed her bridegroom, though she still lives in her father's house[125]. This is why the Song of Songs says: *"A garden enclosed Is my sister, my spouse, A spring shut up, A fountain sealed." (Songs 4:12).* We see the bride here appointed to her bridegroom who bought her, so she cannot

---

123 James Strong: S.T.D.,LL.D., A Concise Dictionary of the word in the Hebrew Bible with their Renderings, Abingdon Press, 1890, P 55.

124 Mendell Lewittes: Jewish Marriage, Rabbinic Law, Legend, and Custom, Jason Aronson Inc., 1994, P 67.

125 Philip and Hanna Goodman: The Jewish Marriage anthology, The Jewish Publication Society of America, 1971, P 75.

look to another, but she must possess simple eyes such as doves *"You have dove's eyes." (Songs 1:15)*, as the doves focus their vision in one direction and do not get distracted by their surroundings[126]. The dove is also a symbol of the Holy Spirit[127], it is as though the Bridegroom wants to say to his bride: "Whenever I look into your eyes, in them I see the work of the Holy Spirit who makes you "תשדוקמ" "Holy" to me. And whenever I look into your eyes, in them I see the reflection of my own image".

2. 2- Perhaps it was easy for the bride in ancient Israel to keep the bridegroom in her heart for a couple of months after he leaves. But when he is late and slows in his return, she starts to wonder. Will my bridegroom keep his word to me and return? Why has he not returned yet? Did he forget about me? This is what the church, the bride of Jesus, may be tried with. That is why Saint Peter the apostle said: *"knowing this first: that scoffers will come in the last days, walking according to their own lusts, and saying, "Where is the promise of His coming? For since the fathers fell asleep, all things continue as they were from the beginning of creation" (2 Peter 3: 3-4).*

3. 3- In this trying time and while the bride is awaiting his return, she must prepare herself[128] and stay loyal and spiritually awake. Let us imagine what the bride would do during this, perhaps extended, waiting period as she waits for her bridegroom who is now her central preoccupation:

---

126 S.J. Hill: Burning Desire, The Story of God's Jealous Love for You, Relevant Media Group inc., 2005, P 127.

127 Look at (Matthew 3:16) "When He had been baptized, Jesus came up immediately from the water; and behold, the heavens were opened to Him, and He saw the Spirit of God descending like a dove and alighting upon Him."

128 Barney Kadsan: God's Appointed Customs/ A Messianic Jewish Guide to the Biblical Lifecycle and Lifestyle, Messianic Jewish Publishers, 1996, P 51.

a. a) She communicates with her bridegroom. She tries to speak with him in every possible way (directly or through messages) and on every occasion which brings them together, she does not see but him. Regardless of how many surround her, she would not want to speak to anyone but him. When she speaks with him, she thanks him for everything he has done for her, she thanks him for the price he paid for her and for his gifts. She also reminds him of his promises, that she is waiting for him, and that she believes every word he had said. Lastly, she asks him to return as soon as possible to take her with him as she is eagerly awaiting this day.

- This is exactly what the church does in her prayer for her Heavenly Bridegroom, whether in personal or communal prayers. She thanks Him, praises Him, reminds Him of His promises, declares her faith in Him and asks for His quick return. This is the reason for which, in every prayer, she rehearses the Nicene Creed saying: "We look for the resurrection of the dead and the life of the age to come. Amen."[129]

- Prayer, then, is communication between a loving bride and Her beloved Bridegroom. As a lover meets his beloved and loses all sense of time, the human soul also would pray to her Heavenly Bridegroom and lose all sense of time spent in His presence, no matter how long. It had been said about Saint Arsenius, teacher of kings' sons, that he used to go outside of his cell on Sunday eves and stand under the sky with the sun behind him, his hands lifted up for prayer until the sun shone on his face.[130]

---

[129] From the orthodox creed of faith.

[130] Monks in the Shehet Wilderness: Fathers' paradise / The Expanded Garden of the Monks / Part One - Delta Press - Fourth Edition - 2010 - p. 631.

- When the bride meets her Heavenly Bridegroom, she pours out all her longing and yearning, thus her eyes tear to wash her heart. This is why the soul prays saying: "Give me, O Lord, many fountains of tears, as you once gave to the sinful woman. And make me worthy to wet your feet, which have freed me from a deviant path, and offer you a superb fragrance, and provide me with a pure life in exchange for repentance."[131]

b. When the bride is in the presence of her bridegroom, she eats joyfully. However, when he leaves, and they bring her food, she would say: "I do not have an appetite for food! How do you want me to think of any delight when I am away from him? He is my only source of pleasure! I cannot think of any food, however delicious it may be, all my thoughts concern my bridegroom and he is more delicious than honey *"His mouth is most sweet, Yes, he is altogether lovely..." (Songs 5:16)*. Furthermore, I am satiated with my bridegroom and *"A satisfied soul loathes the honeycomb..." (Proverbs 27:7)*].

- Jesus, with His pure words, clarified this when He said, all glory be unto Him, answering the questions of John the Baptist's disciples regarding fasting: *"... Can the friends of the Bridegroom mourn as long as the Bridegroom is with them? But the days will come when the Bridegroom will be taken away from them, and then they will fast." (Matthew 9:15)*.

- This is what the church does through her various fasts. Some may marvel at the length of the fasts throughout the year, but when the church, the bride, fasts, she is completely focused

---

[131] From the second service in the midnight prayer, according to the rite of the Coptic Orthodox Church.

on her Bridegroom, she cannot think of any earthly food for all her thinking is about Him, through, Him, and in Him.

- Here, Jesus assures that when the Bridegroom is present with his bride, it is a special situation. For example, the Jewish man was required to put phylacteries on his forehead and his hands during his daily prayer, afterwards, he was required to pray the "Shema"[132]. However, the bridegroom, the groomsman and the friends of the bridegroom were all exempt from these latter requirements as the Babylonian Talmud says: "The teachers of the law said: "The bridegroom, the groomsman and the friends of the bridegroom are all exempted from the prayer and phylacteries, but they are all required to pray the 'Shema'". Similarly, in many churches, the sacrament of marriage is not held during the fasts[133]. As this time is allocated for repentance and humbling oneself before God.

c. c) The bride will speak to whoever visits her during her waiting period about her bridegroom and not about anything else. She will say: "Behold, how beautiful is my bridegroom! Behold, how much he loves me! Look at his precious gifts".

- This is what the church, the bride does. For she speaks of her Bridegroom to the whole world all of the time. Here, she is announcing, like the Apostolic Fathers, the good news through her preaching and evangelism[134]. Evangelism

---

[132] To learn more about the Shema prayer, see Chapter 1, The Bridegroom in Jewish Prayers

[133] The sacrament of marriage is not held during fasting days in the Coptic Orthodox Church, the Greek Orthodox Church, and the Catholic Church. As for the Syriac Church, it is forbidden to hold wedding wreaths during the fasts of Christmas, Nineveh, the first week of the Holy Forty fast and Holy Week, and only in compelling cases is the archbishop of the diocese the right to authorize the making of wreaths in the fasting of the Apostles and the Virgin.

[134] This is what we say in every liturgy: "Amen. Amen. Amen. By your death, O Lord, we preach, and by your holy resurrection and your ascension to the heavens, we confess. We praise you, we bless you, we thank you, O Lord, and we pray to you, our God" – from the liturgy of the Divine Liturgy of St. Basil the Great, according to the rite of the Coptic Church Orthodox.

simply is a wonderful experience lived by the bride with her Heavenly Bridegroom, and out of the wonder of this experience, she cannot stay silent, she goes to everyone around her, saying with Prophet David: ***"Oh, taste and see that the Lord is good…" (Psalm 34:8).***

d. When Satan puts the church on trial and fights her with the thoughts that her Bridegroom is not returning or that he forgot about her, the church runs and brings the marriage contract (Ketuba) and reads the promises in it, so she is strengthened in her spiritual warfare, relying on her ketuba saying: "My Bridegroom has promised me that He will forever remember me, He will protect me, He will love me. He promised to come back to take me and that He will be faithful until the end. All of this is written in the contract".

- This is what the church does continuously as she reads her Ketuba (The Holy Bible which contains the promises and commandments of her Bridegroom). She believes in the efficacy of the word of God as a weapon against the whiles of the devil. This is why no Christian worship is complete without reading the Holy Bible with its two testaments. When the church, the bride reads her ketuba, she does not only read it but she interprets it, teaches it and works to fulfill it.

e. e) If the bridegroom asks his bride during this waiting period: "what do you want?" She would say: "I just want you! Nothing else but you." And this answer would delight the bridegroom's heart very much, so he would give his bride more than she could ever ask for. If king Solomon had given the Queen of Yemen everything she asked for and even more out of overflowing generosity ***"Now King Solomon gave the queen of Sheba all she desired, whatever she asked, besides what Solomon had given her according to*** *the royal generosity..." (1 Kings 10:13)*, then the Heavenly Bridegroom would give much more *"...and indeed a greater than Solomon is here." (Luke 11:31)*

- This is what we do, when we ask of our Heavenly Bridegroom, we seek Him Himself. We ask that He may come to take His bride to live with Him forever. He does not want earthly things to be the focus of our prayers as He knows them very well, that is why He said to us: *"Therefore do not worry, saying, 'What shall we eat?' or 'What shall we drink?' or 'What shall we wear?' For after all these things the Gentiles seek. For your heavenly Father knows that you need all these things. But seek first the kingdom of God and His righteousness, and all these things shall be added to you. Therefore, do not worry about tomorrow, for tomorrow will worry about its own things. Sufficient for the day is its own trouble" (Mathew 6:31-34).*

f. f) When the bride sees the bridegroom's mother, any relative or friend of the bridegroom's, she would certainly ask them to remind the bridegroom of her and her state. She sees in every one of them the image of the bridegroom himself, so she treats them with all respect, love, and reverence.

- This is what the church does when she asks for the saints' intercession. Since she sees the Bridegroom in them and smells His fragrant aroma in them, she speaks with the saints, the Bridegroom's beloved, so that they may speak with Him concerning her, her requests, and her needs. This happens the most with the Mother of her Bridegroom, the Mother of God, the Holy Saint Mary whose intercession the church requests along with a great cloud of witnesses to help her persevere in her fight and spiritual warfare. Our teacher the apostle Saint Paul explained this, saying: *"Therefore we also, since we are surrounded by so great a cloud of witnesses, let us lay aside every weight, and the sin which so easily ensnares us, and let us run with endurance the race that is set before us" (Hebrews 12:1)* We may be surrounded by weakness, weighing down our soul, and we may be attacked by sinful thoughts from every side, this is why we should persevere without ceasing, obedient to the Bridegroom's beloved, following their example in their witnessing to the Bridegroom. This cloud is "ours", not only as an example to be followed by the bride, but it is "ours" as a support in our prayers and communication with the Bridegroom on our behalf.

g. g) What would happen to the bride if she is told to leave her bridegroom? Would she agree? Of course not. But what if she is threatened? If she is tortured? If she is seduced to leave him? Would she agree? No, she would say: "He gave me great love and a precious dowry on the cross, so I cannot leave Him even if I must give up my life."

- This is what the martyrs and confessors did when they refused to deny their soul's true Bridegroom, Jesus Christ. Their sufferings became proof of their consecration to their Bridegroom and a sign of their love for Him.

- This is also what all the monks and cross bearers who lived in the deserts, mountains, caves and cracks of the earth did for their love for their Bridegroom, Jesus. The same thing that is done by the servants and the consecrated when they leave the earthly pleasures and dedicate their life to serving the Bridegroom.

h. h) The bride, at that time, used to make her bridal clothes herself, there were obviously no shops to sell ready-to-wear clothes. For this reason, she had to spend days and months embroidering her wedding dress, so that she may look beautiful on the night of her wedding[135]. The bride knew that she would have to leave everything in her father's house and only take her clothes with her. For her clothes are the only thing that she can carry with her to her Bridegroom's house as she would not need anything there.

- This is what the human soul, which takes months and years preparing her wedding clothes and decorating it with virtues which require much sweat and tears, and spiritual striving. She knows that she will leave everything here, in her father's house (on earth), and go to her Bridegroom only with her clothes (actions)[136].

4. Finally, the Holy Spirit is the One who leads the church, the Christ's Bride, in that difficult time while waiting for her Bridegroom. As we read in the Holy Bible about the bride Esther, King Xerxe's Bride, who left herself to Hege the king's chamberlain to ornament her and prepare her for him[137], so the church surrenders herself to the work of the Holy Spirit to prepare and ornament her while she is waiting for His return. The Holy Spirit is the One who sanctifies the Church, the Bride (this also applies to the human soul), and makes her holy unto the Bridegroom, so the bride stays in the world but is not from the world[138] as she belongs to her Heavenly Bridegroom.

---

[135] Ken Kessler: Understanding the Bride of Christ, Life school International, 2010, P 20.

[136] Look at (Rev 14:13) "Then I heard a voice from heaven saying to me, "Write: 'Blessed are the dead who die in the Lord from now on.' " "Yes," says the Spirit, "that they may rest from their labors, and their works follow them." And look at (Isiah 61:10) "For He has clothed me with the garments of salvation, He has covered me with the robe of righteousness."

[137] Look at "Each young woman's turn came to go into King Ahasuerus after she had completed twelve months' preparation, according to the regulations for the women, for thus were the days of their preparation apportioned: six months with oil of myrrh, and six months with perfumes and preparations for beautifying women" (Esther 2:12)

[138] Revise (John5:19) "If you were of the world, the world would love its own. Yet because you are not of the world, but I chose you out of the world, therefore the world hates you."

Prayer: My Heavenly Prince... my tears are honest feelings melted into drops. I truly love you, and that is why the hours I spend with you in prayer, fasting, and reading the Bible make me feel happy as I speak to you with all that is within me and listen to your tender voice. I will not make an earthly request, but I will seek You as I say along with Prophet David in the psalm: *"Whom have I in heaven but You? And there is none upon earth that I desire besides You" (Psalm 73:25).* Because You are my one desire, when I meet anyone, I would still be focused on You alone and I will tell him about You. No matter how long I wait, it would not compare to the eternal joy I would have with You. Life, no matter how long it lasts, must surely come to an end, but my eternal life with You is my true life.

The Bridegroom's Return

Now, the bridegroom will come to take his bride. Jesus spoke about this step in the parable of "The Ten Virgins" (Mathew 25), that is why explaining this step will help us understand this important parable.

1. The bride in ancient Israel did not have any idea of the day or the hour of the bridegroom's return to take her to his father's house[139]. As the bridegroom's father was the one to decide the date when everything is ready and the bridal home is arranged. When the time is right and complete[140].

2. What usually used to happen was that the bridegroom returned to take his bride late in the night, near midnight when the night is so quiet and sleeping is pleasant. This is also the time when thieves would come as everyone is asleep[141].

---

139 Renald E. Showers: Maranatha, Our Lord Come, The Friends of Israel Gospel Ministry, 1995, P 165.

140 Look at (Mark 13:32) "But of that day and hour no one knows, not even the angels in heaven, nor the Son, but only the Father."

141 Look at (Rev 16:15) "I am coming as a thief." And also look at "For you yourselves know perfectly that the day of the Lord so comes as a thief in the night." (1 Thessalonians 5:2)

3. At the bridegroom's arrival, the sound of רָפוֹשׁ – Shofar would ring out, an old musical instrument usually made from a goat's horn and was used in many traditional religious and social Jewish ceremonies[142]. The sound of the trumpet used to break the silence of the night. Shouting in the streets was heard and a convoy with lanterns heading toward the bride's house was seen. Perhaps this gave the bride a little bit of time for final arrangements. We read in the parable of the ten virgins about the shouting at midnight: *"And at midnight a cry was heard: 'Behold, the Bridegroom is coming; go out to meet him!" (Mathew 25:6)*[143], where we see the bride and those who are with her preparing their lanterns to leave.

4. When the bride knows that her bridegroom is coming, she prepares herself to get in the Palanquin (וְיִרְפַּא-appiryôn), which is a covered caravan for one passenger and is composed of a large box carried on two horizontal sticks by four or six people and it was mentioned in Song of Songs that *"Solomon the King, Made himself a palanquin: He made its pillars of silver, Its support of gold, Its seat of purple, Its interior paved with love By the daughters of Jerusalem" (Song 3: 9,10).*

5. The bride also goes to her bridegroom's house in a big convoy on the palanquin, surrounded by musicians, singers, dancers, friends, relatives, and many guests, and around the palanquin also marched the bride's friends carrying their lanterns to light the way of the convoy in the midst of the dark night. Naturally, there was no time to buy anything such as oil for lanterns, for example[144].

---

[142] Ken Kessler: Understanding the Bride of Christ, Lifeschool International, 2010, P 18.

[143] The word cry here reminds us of the words of the Bible about John the Baptist in (Mark 1:3) "The voice of one crying in the wilderness: 'Prepare the way of the Lord; Make His paths straight.'"

[144] Revise The Parable of the Wise and Foolish Virgins (Matthew 25)

The bridegroom and the bride's voice was heard with this huge convoy in the streets of Jerusalem as said by Prophet Jeremiah: *"Thus says the Lord ... in the streets of Jerusalem ... the voice of joy and the voice of gladness, the voice of the Bridegroom and the voice of the bride, the voice of those who will say: "Praise the Lord of hosts, For the Lord is good, For His mercy endures forever ..." (Jeremiah 33: 10,11).*

And the first book of Maccabees tells us about these rituals saying: *"... were about to celebrate an important wedding and that there would be a bridal procession from the town of Nadabath ... They kept watch and saw a noisy crowd loaded down with baggage. The Bridegroom, his friends, and his relatives were on their way to meet the bride's party. They were heavily armed and were playing musical instruments and drums" (1 Maccabees 9: 37,39) (GNT)*

The bride used to be given much attention at that time, in fact, the Jewish laws say that if two students sat to study the Torah[145] and the bride's convoy passed by them and there were not many people among it, they had to stand up and shout to salute that bride.

Once upon a time, Rabi "Judah son of Elijah" was sitting with his students teaching them and a bride came by, it was only that he stopped the lesson and took a branch from a myrtle tree (Odorous plant) and he kept saluting the bride until she disappeared from his sight. And the Torah justifies these actions as God Himself took care of Eve and brought her to Adam (Gen 2:22), so everyone should take care of the bride and escort her to meet her bridegroom[146].

---

[145] The study of the Torah is very important in Judaism and is usually given the highest priority over anything else.

[146] Philip and Hanna Goodman: The Jewish Marriage anthology, The Jewish Publication Society of America, 1971, P28.

Christ Returns to Take the Bride

6. The Jewish bride used to wear a veil (cover her head with a veil)[147]. From behind the curtain (the palanquin's cover), the bridegroom used to lift his bride's veil to make sure he brought the right bride[148] and this custom is called זְקעדאב - Badeken, which means "Lifting the veil". At this time the bride dazzles beautifully as she is dressed in the most magnificent clothes and the most expensive jewelry and when the veil is lifted, she can see her bridegroom.

7. 7- When the time comes, our Heavenly Bridegroom will come to take us as well. And we will hear the voice of shouting and the sound of the trumpet and it will happen fast in the middle of the night of human history when everyone is asleep (not expecting it nor paying attention)! At that time, there will not be enough time to get ready, so we must be ornamented with virtues and live a life of readiness and spiritual wakefulness: *"Watch, therefore, for you know neither the day nor the hour in which the Son of Man is coming" (Mathew 25:13).*

8. 8- Saint Paul the apostle clarified this step when the Heavenly Bridegroom will come to take His bride saying: *"For the Lord Himself will descend from heaven with a shout, with the voice of an archangel, and with the trumpet of God. And the dead in Christ will rise first. Then we who are alive and remain shall be caught up together with them in the clouds to meet the Lord in the air. And thus we shall always be with the Lord" (1 Thessalonians 4: 16-17).* Here, we clearly see that the Heavenly Bridegroom is coming to take His bride by Himself, where the voice of the Archangel (the shout) and the sound of the trumpet. The bride will be taken

---

147 Refer to what Rebekah did in (Genesis 24:65) where she "... took the burqa and covered herself"; (Genesis 24:64) When she saw Isaac from afar.

148 Refer to the story of Jacob's marriage to Leah and Rachel in (Genesis 29) to understand why this custom entered the Jewish marriage ritual, as Jacob was deceived into marrying Leah instead of Rachel.

in the cloud (the palanquin), then she meets the Lord (as the veil is lifted from her face so she can see him) and stays with Him forever.

9. 9- The carriers of the palanquin remind us of the angels that carry the soul to meet her Heavenly Bridegroom as mentioned in **Luke 16:22: *"So it was that the beggar died, and was carried by the angels to Abraham's bosom. The rich man also died and was buried."*** At this time, the soul, the bride, will be the center of all of heaven's attention.

10. 10- The moment the bride will meet the Bridegroom will be joyful for the bride who is ready (wise), but for the lazy bride (foolish) it will be a terrifying moment! That is why the martyrs were not afraid of dying, because death will take them rapidly to meet their Bridegroom and earn their crowns as: "And God will wipe away every tear from their eyes; there shall be no more death, nor sorrow, nor crying. There shall be no more pain, for the former things have passed away" (Rev 21:4). Concerning this moment, Pope Tawadros the second says in a sermon about the martyrs: "Perhaps when we look into their eyes, what were they seeing? Their eyes were fixed on the sky as if the sky summoned them and was preparing to receive them... These eyes were not the eyes of the body, but the eyes of the elevated heart. We all experienced the taste of a long awaited meeting after a long period of longing, imagine what it would be like in the Divine Presence, united with the righteous, and the saints whose dwelling place has become heaven, what a delightful meeting this is! And this meeting is not like earthly encounters that begin and end... It is an enduring meeting, for in eternity, is without time]"[149].

---

149 Pope Tawadros II: A Lesson from a Sermon / Part Three (41-60) - Monastery of the Great Martyr Marmina al-Ajabi Press in Mariout - 2016 AD - pp. 91-92.

Prayer: My Heavenly Bridegroom... the greatest philosophers and the most fluent authors would not be able to describe this moment upon meeting you. For this is the moment which I have lived for all of my life. But, will you find me ready then? Will you really see me as beautiful? This time, you will come as a just judge. Then, wake up from laziness, O my soul. Perhaps you may hear His voice, saying: *"... Rise up, my love, my fair one, And come away. For lo, the winter is past, The rain is over and gone" (Song 2: 10,11)*

The Bridal Chamber and the Canopy

1. This step is the core of the second part of the Jewish wedding tradition and is called חֻפָּה - Chûppâh –the "Bridal Chamber" and is considered the second part of the wedding rituals where the bridegroom takes his bride to his father's house to live with him in a chamber he prepared there for her. It was mentioned in the Bible over many instances, like: "Which is like a bridegroom coming out of his chamber..." (Psalm 19:5). Also: "Gather the people, Sanctify the congregation, Assemble the elders, Gather the children and nursing babes; Let the bridegroom go out from his chamber, And the bride from her dressing room" (Joel 2:16). This rite is also called the "Nissuin" which means "carries"[150] as well as the "Huppah" which means "lifts".

2. And the word "lifts" is the same word used to describe the divine protection in Isaiah: *"then the Lord will create above every dwelling place of Mount Zion, and above her assemblies, a cloud and smoke by day and the shining of a flaming fire by night. For over all the glory there will be a covering (חֻפָּה)" (Isaiah 4:5),* which means that this ritual is also a protection for the bride, as she is with her bridegroom and nothing bothers her.

---

150 Barney Kadsan: God's Appointed Customs/ A Messianic Jewish Guide to the Biblical Lifecycle and Lifestyle, Messianic Jewish Publishers, 1996, P 51.

3. In the book of Tobias, we see a Jewish bridegroom (Tobias) marrying a Jewish lady (Sarah daughter of Jethro) whose previous seven husbands were killed on the wedding night because of an evil spirit. That is why an angel helped Tobias and rescued him from certain death, asking him to burn the cod liver inside the bridal chamber to defeat Satan (Tobias 6: 10-22).

4. The Mishnah[151] requires the Jewish bridegroom to choose a close friend to be his best man[152]. This friend is the one who testifies as a witness to the marriage and is called the "best man"[153]. He also has a role in helping the bridegroom in the wedding rituals, such as carrying the wedding ring or leading the people in reciting the Seven Blessings (will be detailed later). On the important role of the best man, Rabi Jeremiah son of Eliezer commentates on the verse *"Then the rib which the Lord God had taken from man He made into a woman, and He brought her to the man." (Genesis 2:22)*: "This teaches us that God took on the role of Adam's best man"[154] This, then, is the most important role of the best man, to bring the bride to her bridegroom, afterward, his role is finished, and the bridegroom becomes the center of attention.

5. The bridegroom used to arrive at the bridal chamber before his bride to receive her and welcome her to the place prepared especially for her. The newlyweds then salute the guests gathering in the father's house and afterward they enter their

---

151 Sanhedrin 3 : 5. All the translations from the Mishnah are from The Mishnah, trans. Herbert Danby, Oxford University Press, 1933.

152 He is one of the male attendants accompanying the groom at wedding parties. The best man is usually chosen by the groom himself, and he is often among his friends or people close to him and is called in English (Best Man). (Maids of Honor).

153 J. Rabbinowitz: Midrash Rabbah, The Soncino Press, 1961, P 87.

154 Rabbi Dr. I. Epstein: The Babylonian Talmud/Seder Zera'im, The Soncino Press, 1948, 61a, P 383.

chamber and the bridegroom's friend waits at the door of the chamber until he hears the bridegroom's voice saying that marriage is done. And this is what John the Baptist pointed out when he said: *"He who has the bride is the Bridegroom; but the friend of the bridegroom, who stands and hears him, rejoices greatly because of the bridegroom's voice. Therefore, this joy of mine is fulfilled." (John 3:29)*. Here John the Baptist proclaims to his Jewish audience who were familiar with these marriage rituals that he is just the Bridegroom's friend, not the Bridegroom Himself, that is why he is not the center of attention, since the Bridegroom has arrived. He brings the bride to her bridegroom and rejoices in the bridegroom's joy and with this, his mission ends and his joy is complete.

6. Meanwhile, the guests are celebrating the wedding for a whole week and this celebration is called the "wedding week" and it was the one mentioned in Jacob's marriage to Leah and Rachel: *"And Laban said, "It must not be done so in our country, to give the younger before the firstborn. Fulfill her week, and we will give you this one also for the service which you will serve with me still another seven years." Then Jacob did so and fulfilled her week. So he gave him his daughter Rachel as wife also." (Gen 29: 26-28)*.

7. With the evolution of society, the wedding traditions changed for the bride no longer lives in the bridegroom's father's house. That is why the bridal chamber was replaced with a shade or a canopy. This shade was made of a square piece of silk or velvet and anchored on four pillars and carried by four men. It is open from on all four sides, resembling the openness of the mind and heart of the newlyweds. It used to be embroidered and ornamented with Jewish symbols and some make it out of flowers today. In the past, the pillars

which held the shade were made from trees planted on the day the bridegroom and his bride were born (usually if the newborn was a male, the parents planted a cedar tree and if the newborn was a female, they planted a pine tree)[155].

8. Then, some prayers called "תוכרב עבש – Sheva" or "The Seven Blessings" are recited and they have been used for hundreds of years and the first blessing among them is recited when the second cup of wine is drunk, which seals all the wedding rituals. This prayer says:

First Blessing: Blessed are You O Lord our God, King of the universe, who brings forth the fruit of the vine (the 2nd cup's blessing)

Second Blessing: Blessed are You O Lord our God, King of the universe, who created all things for His glory.

Third Blessing: Blessed are You O Lord our God, King of the universe, Creator of man.

Fourth Blessing: Blessed are You O Lord our God, King of the universe, who created man in His image and likeness, Who Himself prepared for him, an eternal dwelling place. Blessed are You O Lord the Creator of man.

Fifth Blessing: May the barren one [Jerusalem] rejoice and be happy at the gathering of her children around her joyfully. Blessed are You O Lord, who gladdens Zion with her children.

Sixth Blessing: Grant abundant joy to these lovers, as You once bestowed gladness upon Your creation in the Garden of Eden. Blessed are You O Lord, who gladdens the groom and bride.

Seventh Blessing: Blessed are You O Lord our God, King of the

---

[155] Encyclopaedia Judaica: Second Edition/Volume 13, Keter Publishing House Ltd., 2007, P 568.

universe, who created joy and happiness, the groom and bride, gladness and jubilation, cheer and delight, love, friendship, harmony, and fellowship. O Lord our God, let us soon hear in the cities of Judah and in the streets of Jerusalem the sounds of joy and happiness, the sound of the groom and the sound of the bride, the sound of exultation of newlyweds from under their shade, the sound of the youths in hymns of feasts. Blessed are You O Lord, who gladdens the groom with his bride.

9. Although the first blessing is to bless the cup of wine, and it is the introduction to the other blessings, the cup is not drunk except after reciting the other prayers.

10. It is worth mentioning that, and after drinking from the cup, the bridegroom breaks it with his feet and all the invitees shout "בוט לזמ". This happens to express the grief of all the Jews when the temple was destroyed in Jerusalem.

Here, we see everyone in their greatest moments of joy with the newlyweds remembering an incident that causes sadness (the temple's destruction) as if they prefer Jerusalem to this joyful moment, saying along with David the Prophet and king: *"If I do not exalt Jerusalem Above my chief joy." (Psalm 137: 6)*. This is a brief foreshadowing of the newlyweds' life together, where joy is found alongside sadness as life is a mixture of both at once.

This is why the Jewish Rabbis were careful to moderate joy during weddings. The Talmud narrates that when Rabbi "Ashi" held his son's wedding ceremony, he noticed that the attendees were exaggerating in happiness, so he took a precious cup of white glass and broke it in front of them, which made them grieve. This is also what "Bin Rabina" did when he broke a cup worth 400 silver coins, which made the guests feel sorrow.[156]

---

[156] Goldwurm, Hersh, Nosson Scherman, Yisroel S. Schorr, and Chaim Malinowitz. Talmud Bavli: [talmud Bavli] : the Schottenstein Edition : the Gemara : the Classic Vilna Edition, with an Annotated, Interpretive Elucidation, As an Aid to Talmud Study. , 1990.

Christ the Bridegroom

11. The bridal chamber was a symbol of God's meeting with his people, this is why we see in the Jewish tradition that the bridal chamber was designed to resemble the Holy of Holies in the meeting tent. Of that, one of the Rabbis says: "If a father asks a friend of his to build a marriage room (hajla) for his son, he must build it four cubits by six cubits." As Rabbi Ismael says: " Its height should be half its length and half its width." The Holy of Holies proves this. Additionally, Rabbi Simon bin Gamaliel says: "The building must be identical with the building of the Holy of Holies". Concerning the decoration of the chamber, Jewish tradition says: "As the tent was decorated with all colors, so was the tent of meeting decorated with all colors, blue, purple, scarlet, and fine linen" (Exodus 25:4), "and her spices spread" (Song 4:16). And the Babylonian Talmud says: "If the husband and wife are deserving, then the Divine Presence dwells with them"[157]. It is worth noting that conservative Jews at their wedding ceremonies design the canopy (the dome) to resemble the tent of meeting[158].

12. The bridal chamber in the ancient Jewish tradition or the shade in its modern counterpart is a symbol of heaven, it is the place where the bridegroom meets his bride and where he lifts (from the word Huppah) his bride from earth to her heavenly home to live with her bridegroom in everlasting joy. She would be with him on her own. Meanwhile, God's rage is poured on the evil ones. And this is what Prophet Isaiah meant when he said: *"Come, my people, enter your*

Print. Berakhot 31a and 30b.

157 Goldwurm, Hersh, Nosson Scherman, Yisroel S. Schorr, and Chaim Malinowitz. Talmud Bavli: [talmud Bavli] : the Schottenstein Edition : the Gemara : the Classic Vilna Edition, with an Annotated, Interpretive Elucidation, As an Aid to Talmud Study. , 1990. Print. Sotah 17a.

158 Brant Pitre: Jesus the Bridegroom/The Greatest Love Story Ever Told,First Edition, 2014, P 92-93.

chambers, And shut your doors behind you; Hide yourself, as it were, for a little moment, Until the indignation is past. For behold, the Lord comes out of His place To punish the inhabitants of the earth for their iniquity..." (Isaiah 26: 20,21).

13. The Bride and the guests are in a state of continuous joy due to the wedding. Despite this beauty, there are some who refuse to come to the wedding. Yes, there are those who are stubborn, hardening their hearts, or ignore the invitation. By doing so, without knowing, they reject the true joy which is in the presence of Christ the Bridegroom. This is the condition of those who are away from God and His church. And about this is what His Holiness Pope Shenouda III says, in a poem entitled "How to Forget"[159] :

How many days did the Lord call me and I turned away from Him
And He showed me His tender heart, I am the one running away from Him
He said, "Be a chest to my heart, but I was not."
My heart in my chest was like a rock, it was harder
He said, O friend of my wedding, will you attend, so I apologized
He repeated the words in kindness and sympathy, and I became bored
He stopped after saying "wait for me", I did not wait
There was no longing in my heart to attend a wedding

14. What is more difficult than this, is that those who have not come to the wedding will be in a state of anger and discontent with the Bridegroom. That is why Zephaniah the prophet said: *"The great day of the Lord is near; It is near and hastens quickly. The noise of the day of the Lord is bitter; There the*

---

[159] Pope Shenouda III: The Initiation of the Spirit - Anba Royce Press - Eighth Edition / 1993 AD - pp. 146 - 147.

mighty men shall cry out. That day is a day of wrath, A day of trouble and distress, A day of devastation and desolation, A day of darkness and gloominess, A day of clouds and thick darkness, A day of trumpet and alarm Against the fortified cities and against the high towers. "I will bring distress upon men, and they shall walk like blind men, because they have sinned against the Lord; Their blood shall be poured out like dust, And their flesh like refuse." (Zephaniah 1: 14-17). In the parable of the wedding of the king's son, when those invited refused to attend the wedding and they caught the king's servants and insulted them and killed them, they deserved severe punishment, as it was mentioned in ***Matthew 22:7: "But when the king heard about it, he was furious. And he sent out his armies, destroyed those murderers, and burned up their city."***

15. As for the seven days that the bride spends with her bridegroom and the guests celebrate, they resemble **a joyful eternity in abundance and perfection.** As the number seven is often used in the Bible as an **indication of abundance.** We see it clearly in the vengeance of Cain "sevenfold" (Gen. 4:15), fleeing in seven ways (Deut. 28:7) deliverance from seven troubles (Job 5:19), praising God **seven** times a day (Psalm 119:164), and in *"The words of the Lord are pure words, like silver tried in a furnace of earth, Purified seven times." (Psalm 12:6),* and in *"And if he sins against you seven times in a day, and seven times in a day returns to you, saying, 'I repent,' you shall forgive him" (Luke 17:4).* We find it also in the **seven** requests in the Lord's prayer (Matthew 6: 9-13), the **seven** parables of the kingdom of heaven (Matthew 13), the **seven** woes for the Pharisees (Matthew 23: 13, 15, 16, 23, 25, 27, 29), the **seven** gifts of the Holy Spirit (Romans 12: 6-9), and the **seven** characteristics of the divine wisdom (James 3: 17).

Furthermore, number seven in the Bible is an indication of perfection and fullness, as the number of the days of the week is **seven** (Gen. 2:2), God warned Noah before the great flood, then **seven** days before the rain and when Noah sent the crow and the dove, that was after **seven** days (Gen. 7: 4, 8: 10,12), the number of the clean animals that entered the ark was **seven** (Gen. 7: 2). In Pharaoh's dream which was interpreted by Joseph, there were **seven** cows and seven **heads** of grains (Gen. 41: 2-7). The Jews used to celebrate the **seventh** day of worship and the **seventh** year, the Jubilee year was **seven** years seven times, and the feasts of the Passover and Sukkot were seven days with **seven** sacrifices. John wrote in the book of Revelation to **seven** churches and saw **seven** lampstands, **seven** spirits, **seven** stamps, **seven** trumpets, **seven** thunders, **seven** bowls, and **seven** plagues. And the number of **sevens** mentioned in the Bible exceeds 600 times.[160]

16. As the bride remembers Jerusalem even in her most joyful moments of the wedding, we should also be concerned with the heavenly Jerusalem and not get distracted with anything else, especially in times of joy.

Prayer: Oh Good Shepherd... whoever takes shelter in You is safe, let me, then, take shelter in You from now on, so when the time of your wrath comes, I would say along with the Song of Song's bride: *"... his banner over me is love" (Song 2: 4).* This flag over me is the shade and canopy that I take shelter in. Let me understand what David said of you in the psalm *"For He is our God, And we are the people of His pasture, And the sheep of His hand. Today, if you will hear His voice: Do not harden your hearts, as in the rebellion, As In the day of trial in the wilderness." (Psalm 95: 7,8).* O God, I am a sheep whose heart has hardened and left His Shepherd. But because of Your love and mercy, You search for me

---

[160] A selection of professors with specializations: The Bible Dictionary - House of the Family Library - 2000 AD - pg 456.

and give me a way to repent and attend the wedding. Open my mind and heart, then, to appreciate your invitation to Your wedding and rejoice with you in heavenly Jerusalem forever.

The Wedding Banquet

1. After the 7 days of the celebration have passed, the bride and the Bridegroom meet with the guests, "sons of the bridechamber"[161] in a joyful celebration, the wedding banquet. This is the first banquet for the bridegroom and his bride with guests and is called "הוצמ תדועס" – Seudat mitzvah" which means "the wedding banquet" and it has a religious purpose as well since it brings joy to the heart of the newlyweds. This custom originated because of Laban, Jacob's father in law who invited all the population to a big banquet when Leah his daughter was married as mentioned in: *"And Laban gathered together all the men of the place and made a feast" (Gen. 29: 22).*

2. The guests wear the best clothes (the wedding clothes)[162] and music is played, especially the trumpet. The guests used to recite poems praising the bridegroom and dance before the newlyweds joyfully.[163]

3. The Jews prohibited work during these days, as well as in other cultures. As the Jewish story of Joseph's marriage from Asenath, the daughter of Poti-Pherah priest of On: "And afterwards Pharaoh made a wedding feast, a huge dinner and great wedding banquet that lasted seven days and he invited to it all the chiefs of Egypt and the kings of the nations. And

---

161 Bani: From the Greek word υἱός, meaning son. Refer to (Matthew 9:15), (Mark 2:19) and (Luke 5:34).

162 Refer to the story of the man who did not wear wedding clothes (Matthew 22:11-13) in the parable of the king's son's wedding.

163 Ken Kessler: Understanding the Bride of Christ, Lifeschool International, 2010, P 20.

it was declared in the land of Egypt that whoever works during the seven days of the wedding feast of Joseph and Asenath will be killed][164].

4. It was not possible for the wedding party to fast in the presence of the bridegroom, this is why Jesus said to disciples of John the Baptist when they came asking: *"Then the disciples of John came to Him, saying, "Why do we and the Pharisees fast often, but Your disciples do not fast?" And Jesus said to them, "Can the friends of the Bridegroom mourn as long as the Bridegroom is with them? But the days will come when the Bridegroom will be taken away from them, and then they will fast" (Mathew 9: 14,15).*

5. There is a direct reference to the wedding banquet in the words of Jesus Christ. When the disciples asked who shall be greater among them, the Teacher clarified to them that the greatest is the one who serves all, like Him. Here, Jesus invited His bride to leave false glory, to carry the cross and to share in His pain to participate with Him in His glories and most of all "The Wedding Banquet". He said: *"But you are those who have continued with Me in My trials. And I bestow upon you a kingdom, just as My Father bestowed one upon Me, that you may eat and drink at My table in My kingdom..." (Mathew 22: 28-30).*

6. We also read about this great heavenly banquet in the book of Revelation which was called the marriage of the Lamb as mentioned in **Revelation 19: 6-9**: *"And I heard, as it were, the voice of a great multitude, as the sound of many waters and as the sound of mighty thundering, saying, "Alleluia! For the Lord God Omnipotent reigns! Let us be glad and*

---

[164] E. W. Brooks: Joseph and Asenath/Translations of Early Documents, Society for Promoting Christian Knowledge, 1918, P 62.

rejoice and give Him glory, for the marriage of the Lamb has come, and His wife has made herself ready." And to her it was granted to be arrayed in fine linen, clean and bright, for the fine linen is the righteous acts of the saints."

7. Who will be invited to the marriage of the Lamb? Of course, and above all, the Theotokos, the Holy Saint Mary along with Abraham, Isaac and Jacob[165], the prophets, the apostles, the evangelists, the martyrs, and all the spirits of the righteous who were complete in faith[166].

8. It is a curious banquet in which people who have lived in different eras and places take part. It is something which exceeds the mind for us to see, face to face, the saints about whom we read and of which we have heard! How would we feel? How much joy would we feel? It is really something beyond explanation. Even the eloquent Saint Paul the apostle could not describe it and said: *"Eye has not seen, nor ear heard, Nor have entered into the heart of man The things which God has prepared for those who love Him"* (1 Co. 2:9).

Prayer: My Heavenly Prince...Truly blessed are those who are invited to the wedding of the lamb. Thank You for preparing this wonderful feast. I cannot imagine that I will see the saints of whom I have read in the Old Testament! What would Abraham, Moses, and Samson look like? Will I have the chance to meet the Virgin Mary, the apostles, the martyrs, and the saints? Will I see all my loved ones who have died in You? What a glorious celebration which includes all the righteous from every generation, where there is no sadness or pain, but a continuous joy which deeply satisfies me so that I need of nothing else.

---

165 Refer to the litany of the departed, "Lord, please, repose all of their souls in the bosom of our holy fathers, Abraham, Isaac and Jacob." It is said in the raising of incense on the evening and early days according to the rite of the Coptic Orthodox Church.

166 From the synod prayer in the Divine Liturgy of Saint Basil the Great, according to the rite of the Coptic Orthodox Church.

Chapter 5

An Inspiration from the Bridegroom and the Bride

This is an attempt to look at some of the events and biblical texts from the real perspective that Jesus Christ is the Bridegroom. It is an attempt to see another dimension to events that we have always read about as Christians, perhaps without digging deep into their Jewish roots. This is why we now need to reread with different eyes... with the eyes of the first century Jews.

Now, allow me, dear reader, to take you on a trip throughout this chapter to get closer to our glorified Lord Jesus Christ. Come along with me to discover who is the true Bridegroom in the wedding of Cana! And let us figure out how He made from Zion's upper room a new Sinai on the night of the secret dinner! Let us see Him as a Bridegroom for the Samaritan and even for all of Samaria! Come along, let us taste His amazing love as the crucified Bridegroom and know His precious dowry for the bride! Let us understand the amazing secret of marriage and the glory of the life of virginity!

The Wedding of Cana

"On the third day there was a wedding in Cana of Galilee, and the mother of Jesus was there. Now both Jesus and His disciples were invited to the wedding. And when they ran out of wine, the mother of Jesus said to Him, "They have no wine." Jesus said to her, "Woman, what does your concern have to do with Me?

My hour has not yet come." His mother said to the servants, "Whatever He says to you, do it."

Now there were set there six water pots of stone, according to the manner of purification of the Jews, containing twenty or thirty gallons apiece. Jesus said to them, "Fill the water pots with water." And they filled them up to the brim. And He said to them, "Draw some out now, and take it to the master of the feast." And they took it.

When the master of the feast had tasted the water that was made wine, and did not know where it came from (but the servants who had drawn the water knew), the master of the feast called the Bridegroom. And he said to him, "Every man at the beginning sets out the good wine, and when the guests have well drunk, then the inferior. You have kept the good wine until now!"

This beginning of signs Jesus did in Cana of Galilee, and [a] manifested His glory; and His disciples believed in Him. After this He went down to Capernaum, He, His mother, His brothers, and His disciples; and they did not stay there many days."

(John 2: 1-12)

1. Let us start by asking: Why had Jesus not started His public ministry on a day other than the day of the wedding of Cana? He could have started it as a teacher in the sermon on the mountain[167], or with a miracle of resurrection at the tomb of Lazarus,[168] or even with the exorcism of Legion[169], the devil in the country of the Gadarenes[170], but He, and all glory be

---

167 Refer to (Matthew 5)

168 Refer to (John 11)

169 Legion: It is a Latin name for the division of the Roman army, which included 6000 soldiers in the days of Augustus Caesar, (6000 infantry, in addition to about 1200 cavalry). And the name here refers to the number of many unclean spirits.

170 Refer to (Mark 5)

unto Him, has not done any of that! But He chose to turn water into wine at a Jewish wedding in Cana of the Galilee to be His first miracle which declares His glory as mentioned in John 2:11:"This **beginning of signs** Jesus did in Cana of Galilee and **manifested His glory**; and His disciples believed in Him." He did this in Cana before revealing His great wisdom as a teacher, and before declaring His absolute power over unclean spirits, and even before He demonstrated His great power as a healer for different diseases.

Beyond that, the Greek expression used by our teacher Saint John the evangelist to describe this miracle is "the beginning of signs" (ἀρχὴν τῶν σημείων - archē ton sēmeion) and the word "ἀρχή" does not just mean "the beginning" but it also means "chief"[171]. That is why this miracle is not just the beginning of signs but it is the "head of the signs" or "the chief sign". Now, we are faced with a chief miracle, but why?

2. To answer this question Pope Tawadros II, may God prolong his life, said: "Jesus Christ describes all the time of His life here on earth as a prolonged wedding feast (Mark 2: 18-20) and that is why He started His public appearance in the wedding feast of Cana"[172]. Now let us ask another question: who was responsible for providing the wine at the wedding? The Bridegroom, of course. Therefore, our Lord made this miracle to simply say **"I am the True Bridegroom."** And to understand that let us go back to the beginning.

3. Saint John the evangelist mentioned at the beginning of the miracle that it was performed on the third day. In fact,

---

171 James Strong: S.T.D.,LL.D., A Concise Dictionary of the word in the Greek Testament, Abingdon Press, 1890, P 16.

172 Pope Tawadros II: The Key to the New Testament / Part One / The Four Good News / Matthew the Messenger, Mark to the Messenger, Luke the Apostle, John the Apostle - Coptic Orthodox Patriarchate and St. Athanasius the Apostolic Seminary, Damanhour - Diocese of Beheira and its dependencies - 2013 AD - p. 218.

the wedding in Cana was on the third day as, on the first day, Jesus invited John, Andrew, and Peter as mentioned in John 1: 35-42 and on the second day, He invited Philip and Nathanael as mentioned in John 1: 43-51. However, if we go a few days prior, we know that this was on the sixth day of the start of His ministry as detailed below:

First day: John the Baptist testifies to Him (John 1:20)

Second day: "The next day John saw Jesus coming toward him, and said, Behold! The Lamb of God who takes away the sin of the world!" (John 1:29)

Third day: Andrew and John followed Him (John 1:40).

Fourth day: Philip and Nathanael followed Him (John 1:45).

Fifth day: The Lord was on a trip to Galilee.

Sixth day: The Lord was at the wedding of Cana[173].

And when a Jewish person hears the word "sixth day", the days of the creation immediately come to mind, remembering the first wedding in all of human history, the wedding of Adam and Eve on the sixth day. So, Christ the Bridegroom makes this important miracle on the sixth day of His ministry to remind us of the wedding in Genesis, the wedding of Adam and Eve.

4. To better understand this, let us ask: why had the Virgin Mary said to Jesus Christ that they do not have any wine while he was just a guest at the wedding and not responsible for it? Is it not strange to tell her son about this problem rather than the master of the feast? Why did Jesus reply: "my time has not come yet"? What is the correlation between "they do not have wine" and "my time has not come yet"? And why did

---

173 Pope Tawadros II: "The previous reference," p. 217.

An Inspiration from the Bridegroom and the Bride

Jesus accept to perform this miracle after all, even after His initial response?

5. To answer these questions, let us go back to the Jewish traditions of marriage and remember that the wedding ceremony did not last for a day or two, but for seven full days[174]. So, if modern-day brides are so meticulous and spend much effort to prepare for a wedding meant to last for a few hours, to take on its best image, how much more would the bride in ancient Israel have done with a wedding that lasts for an entire week? The bride certainly had to spend greater effort and be more careful. But the bride in Cana was not like that, if she had been more careful, the problem would not have happened, and the wine would not have run out!

6. On the other hand, Isaiah the prophet says: *"The new wine fails, the vine languishes, All the merry-hearted sigh... They shall not drink wine with a song; Strong drink is bitter to those who drink it... There is a cry for wine in the streets, All joy is darkened, The mirth of the land is gone." (Isaiah 24: 7, 9, 11).* He clarifies that there is no wine and there is no joy either. But who will fix this? Who will provide the wine? Isaiah the prophet also answers, saying: *"And in this mountain The Lord of hosts will make for all people A feast of choice pieces, A feast of wines on the lees..." (Isaiah 25: 6).* Then when there's no wine, God (Jehovah the Bridegroom of Israel[175]) is the one who provides the wine.

7. In the wedding of Cana, the bride (Israel) was not awake, so her wine had run out. But the Bridegroom (God) brings the wine. Thus, we are not facing a miracle of merely turning

---

174 For more details, see the hopscotch and the parachute in Chapter Four of this book.

175 For more details about Jehovah, the Bridegroom of Israel, see the first and second chapters of this book.

water into wine, though it is an important miracle regarding the theology of the Son incarnate, but we are facing yet another theological dimension, in which Jesus, God, the Lord of Hosts and the source of joy[176], as Prophet Isaiah said of Him in his prophecy which was now fulfilled in the wedding of Cana.

8. This means that when Virgin Mary said: "they ran out of wine," she was really saying: "they ran out of joy". Regarding the role of the Virgin Mary in this miracle Pope Tawadros the II says: "Virgin Mary presented her request to Christ, her son because she has substantial significance:

a. She may have been related to the apparent bridegroom in the wedding of Cana-which represents the Old Testament.

b. She is the real mother of the real Bridegroom in the wedding feast-which represents the New Testament.

She is a "mediator" between both testaments which is why she called Jesus, not only because of the shortage of wine but the shortage of joy that they should have been in"[177].

3. We can then identify Christ the Bridegroom in "Cana of Galilee", for Jesus Christ was not responsible for providing the wine but the bridegroom of Cana was the one in charge. We know that from what happened afterward, as the bible says: "When the master of the feast had tasted the water that was made wine and did not know where it came... the master of the feast called the Bridegroom. And he said to him, "Every man at the beginning sets out the good wine, and when the guests have well drunk, then the inferior. You have kept the

---

[176] Wine is a symbol of joy, see Step Five: The Cup of the Covenant from Chapter Three of this book.

[177] op. cit., 219-220.

good wine until now!" (John 2: 9,10). The bridegroom of Cana did not provide wine, but Jesus Christ was the One who provided it. So, Virgin Mary was not asking him to solve a familial problem in an ordinary wedding ceremony, but she was asking Him to complete His role as a Jewish Bridegroom! She was telling Him that they do not have wine and You, as a Bridegroom, are responsible for providing it. That is why Jesus accepted to play the role of the Bridegroom and He performed the miracle and provided the good wine.

4. Jesus told Mary: *"Woman, what does your concern have to do with Me".* The word woman here is γυνή - gunē in Greek and it corresponds to the Hebrew word הָאִשָּׁה נָשִׁים - ishshâh nâshîym used in Genesis to describe Eve: "This is now bone of my bones and flesh of my flesh; She shall be called Woman because she was taken out of Man" (Gen. 2: 23). The word "woman" here, then, is not an insult but it is a reference to Eve, the very first one to be called "woman". The Virgin Mary here is the new Eve, mother of all the living in spirit. From this we understand that Jesus calls Mary "woman" as a reference to the first wedding, the wedding of Adam and Eve in the book of Genesis. For the Virgin here resembles the church of the New Testament, the bride taken out of the side of Christ, the Bridegroom, who is the second Adam.

5. Christ the Bridegroom will also give wine in the upper room to his disciples on Covenant Thursday. Between the miracle of the wedding of Cana of Galilee and Covenant Thursday there is a long period of time separating them that is why He answered Mary and said: *"My hour has not yet come." (John 2:4).* The Greek word for "an hour" is (ὥρα - hōra) and Jesus used to use it to describe His holy sufferings and which is what we read, for example, in ***John 12:27**: "Now*

Christ the Bridegroom

My soul is troubled, and what shall I say? 'Father, save Me from this hour (ὥρα)'? But for this purpose I came to this hour (ὥρα)." and also in *John 17:1: "Father, the hour (ὥρα) has come. Glorify Your Son, that Your Son also may glorify You".* He also said to His disciples *"... Are you still sleeping and resting? It is enough! The hour (ὥρα) has come; behold, the Son of Man is being betrayed into the hands of sinners." (Mark 14:41).*

6. Thus, Jesus' reply: *"My hour has not yet come." (John 2:4)* means that the hour during which I give the wine of the New Testament has not yet come, my blood which will be poured as mentioned in *Matthew 26: 27-28: "Then He took the cup, and gave thanks, and gave it to them, saying, "Drink from it, all of you. For this is My blood of the new covenant, which is shed for many for the remission of sins."* The close connection between what happened on Covenant Thursday and the hour of suffering is no secret. That is why Saint John the apostle made sure to connect the two events as he said in his book: *"Now before the Feast of the Passover, when Jesus knew that His hour had come that He should depart from this world to the Father, having loved His own who were in the world, He loved them to the end. And supper being ended, the devil having already put it into the heart of Judas Iscariot, Simon's son, to betray Him" (John 13: 1,2).*

7. Christ the Bridegroom appears in this miracle in a different way as the Coptic Synaxarium[178] mentions along with Ibn Kabar[179] regarding Simon the Zealot[180]: "It is said that he

---

178 The Synaxarium: It is a book that contains the biographies of the saints and martyrs, the memorials of the feasts, and the days of fasting, arranged according to the days of the year, and it is read from it in the daily liturgies. It uses the Coptic calendar and the Coptic months (thirteen months).

179 Rev. Shams al-Riyasah Abu al-Barakat, known as Ibn Kabar: The Lamp of Darkness in the Clarification of Service, Part One - Al-Karouz Library - 1971 AD - p. 82.

180 The Coptic Church celebrates it on the 15th of Bashans.

was the bridegroom of the wedding in Cana where Jesus turned water to wine, which made him, after this miracle, leave everything and follow the Redeemer and became one of his disciples." This way, Jesus had turned him from a bridegroom to a bride! Yes, from just an earthly bridegroom into a heavenly bride.

8. Truly, the miracle of the wedding of Cana was as the beginning of unveiling Jesus as the New Testament Bridegroom, but in a Jewish way and through traditional Jewish wedding rituals. That is the reason Jesus started His ministry with this miracle.

The Last Supper

1. Let us read the biblical verses that speak of the last supper and notice the wonderful compatibility between them, especially when speaking of the covenant and the blood.

"Then He took the cup, and gave thanks, and gave it to them, saying, "Drink from it, all of you. For this is My blood of the new covenant, which is shed for many for the remission of sins" (Mathew 26: 27-28).

"And He said to them, "This is My blood of the new covenant, which is shed for many" (Mark 14:24).

"Likewise He also took the cup after supper, saying, "This cup is the new covenant in My blood, which is shed for you" (Luke 22:20).

"In the same manner He also took the cup after supper, saying, "This cup is the new covenant in My blood. This do, as often as you drink it, in remembrance of Me" (1 Co. 11:25).

2. We notice that all these verses identify the cup with the words **"blood"** and **"new covenant"**. Any Jew in the first century

AD (like the disciples of Jesus) upon hearing the words **"covenant" and "blood"** would remember the covenant of "Jehovah" and "Israel" on Mount Sinai at once. To understand this, let us compare the words of Jesus in the last supper with the words of Moses the prophet in Exodus: *"And Moses took the blood, sprinkled it on the people, and said, "This is the blood of the covenant which the Lord has made with you according to all these words" (Exodus 24:8).*

3. This covenant is then as the blood covenant in Sinai, Moses established the covenant by sprinkling the blood of the sacrifices on the people saying: *"This is the blood of the covenant which the Lord has made with you" (Exodus 24:8),* but Jesus took the cup and gave thanks and gave it to his disciples saying: *"Drink from it, all of you. For this is My blood of the new covenant[181]".* But here, Jesus who is God calls it a " new covenant". This new covenant is what the prophet Jeremiah pointed out and referred to:

"Behold, the days are coming, says the Lord, when I will make a new covenant with the house of Israel and with the house of Judah— not according to the covenant that I made with their fathers in the day that I took them by the hand to lead them out of the land of Egypt, My covenant which they broke, though I was a husband to them, says the Lord. But this is the covenant that I will make with the house of Israel after those days, says the Lord: I will put My law in their minds, and write it on their hearts; and I will be their God, and they shall be My people" (Jeremiah 31: 31-33).

4. The tribes of Israel represented Israel, the bride of the Old Testament and now the disciples represent the church, the bride of the New Testament. As "Jehovah" established His Old Testament with Israel on Mount Sinai, Jesus, the

---

[181] Gerges Samuel Azar: The Eucharist / The Good Saying of the Glorious Secret - St. George's Library, Shubra - 1935 AD - p. 76.

An Inspiration from the Bridegroom and the Bride

Bridegroom, established His new covenant in the upper room of Zion. Here, Jesus Christ is not just celebrating a new Passover, but He is establishing a new marriage covenant of which the prophets had long spoken.

5. This way, the upper room of Zion became a new Sinai, greater than the old one, as Christ the Bridegroom established in it a new covenant with his church. Christ the Bridegroom, here, gives the greatest gift to his bride, he gives himself to her (His holy body and blood). Every time we take from His holy blood and body, we remember His new covenant with us and remember His dowry that He paid for us on the cross. That is why the apostle Saint Paul said: ***"For as often as you eat this bread and drink this cup, you proclaim the Lord's death till He comes" (1 Co. 11:26)*** and this is what we acknowledge in the divine liturgy, as the priest says: "Because every time you eat from this bread and drink from this cup you preach my death and proclaim my resurrection and remember me till I come"[182].

6. In the ritual of the divine liturgy of the Coptic Orthodox Church and during the sanctification prayers, the priest carries the bread with both of his hands, so his ten fingers appear carrying the bread that turns into the body of Jesus Christ. Indicating that the One who gave the ten commandments (in the Old Testament) is the same One who is now giving His body (in the New Testament) carried on ten fingers.

7. Saint Augustine said: "Every celebration (of the Eucharist) is a wedding celebration, a celebration of the church's wedding. The King's Son is taking a bride. And the King's Son is a King Himself and the guests are themselves the bride

---

182   From the liturgy of the Divine Liturgy of Saint Basil the Great, according to the rite of the Coptic Orthodox Church.

... as the bride of Jesus is the whole church. And from her the beginning and the first fruit which is the body of Christ. Because there, the Bride was united with her Bridegroom...]"[183].

The Samaritan Woman

1. We see in the New Testament Jesus the Bridegroom very clearly so we wonder: Who may His bride be?

We read in the first chapter about "Jehovah" the Bridegroom and Israel the bride of whom the Bridegroom spoke in *Jeremiah 31:4: "Again I will build you, and you shall be rebuilt, O virgin of Israel ..."* then we read about John the Baptist, the Bridegroom's best man who prepares the bride, Israel, to meet her Bridegroom, Jesus, so he said: *"He who has the bride is the Bridegroom; but the friend of the Bridegroom, who stands and hears him, rejoices greatly because of the Bridegroom's voice. Therefore, this joy of mine is fulfilled" (John 3:29)*. Afterwards, Jesus celebrated a new wedding with His disciples in the upper room of Zion as a reference to the church of the New Testament. With this, the New Testament's bride is like her Old Testament counterpart, not an individual but a group. Thus, she is a whole people. She is from New Israel. She is the Holy Church.

2. We will speak here about what happened at the well of Jacob. But let us first look at what our teacher Saint John the evangelist wrote as inspired by the Holy Spirit with Jewish eyes:

"He (Jesus Christ) left Judea and departed again to Galilee. But He needed to go through Samaria. So He came to a city of Samaria which is called Sychar, near the plot of ground that Jacob gave to his son Joseph. Now Jacob's well was there. Jesus

---
[183] St. Augustin, Lecures or Tractates on the Gospel according to John/ The Nicene and Post Nicene Fathers / Series1 / Volume 7, Books for Ages/ AGES Software, Version 2.0, 1997 – Homily 2, P 934.

An Inspiration from the Bridegroom and the Bride

therefore, being wearied from His journey, sat thus by the well. It was about the sixth hour.

A woman of Samaria came to draw water. Jesus said to her, "Give Me a drink." For His disciples had gone away into the city to buy food. Then the woman of Samaria said to Him, "How is it that You, being a Jew, ask a drink from me, a Samaritan woman?" For Jews have no dealings with Samaritans. Jesus answered and said to her, "If you knew the gift of God, and who it is who says to you, 'Give Me a drink,' you would have asked Him, and He would have given you living water." The woman said to Him, "Sir, You have nothing to draw with, and the well is deep. Where then do You get that living water? Are You greater than our father Jacob, who gave us the well, and drank from it himself, as well as his sons and his livestock?" Jesus answered and said to her, "Whoever drinks of this water will thirst again, but whoever drinks of the water that I shall give him will never thirst. But the water that I shall give him will become in him a fountain of water springing up into everlasting life." The woman said to Him, "Sir, give me this water, that I may not thirst, nor come here to draw." Jesus said to her, "Go, call your husband, and come here." The woman answered and said, "I have no husband." Jesus said to her, "You have well said, 'I have no husband,' for you have had five husbands, and the one whom you now have is not your husband; in that you spoke truly."

The woman said to Him, "Sir, I perceive that You are a prophet. Our fathers worshiped on this mountain, and you Jews say that in Jerusalem is the place where one ought to worship." Jesus said to her, "Woman, believe Me, the hour is coming when you will neither on this mountain, nor in Jerusalem, worship the Father. You worship what you do not know; we know what we worship, for salvation is of the Jews.

But the hour is coming, and now is, when the true worshipers will worship the Father in spirit and truth; for the Father is seeking such to worship Him. God is Spirit, and those who worship Him must worship in spirit and truth." The woman said to Him, "I know that Messiah is coming" (who is called Christ). "When He comes, He will tell us all things." Jesus said to her, "I who speak to you am He." (John 4: 3-26)

3. Let us begin by asking: why would John mention the name of the well "The Well of Jacob" and its location in detail? Why would he mention the time, that it was at the sixth hour of the day? Why did Jesus start a conversation with a Samaritan woman? Do the Jews not see the Samaritans as unholy? Why did He talk to her, then, asking her to give Him water? What is the meaning of this long conversation between them? And why did they talk about the Living Water? Why did the conversation turn from water to the woman's past, then to the place where we should worship God? And more importantly what does this have to do with the topic of the bride and the Bridegroom?

4. In fact, if any Jew read the previous text, he would immediately look to the Samaritan woman as a bride, as the scene of a woman filling her pot of water from a well is a very common and a familiar scene in many Jewish marriages. **As the well was a meeting place for many couples** and here are some examples:

a. **Moses met Zipporah at a well:** *"When Pharaoh heard of this matter, he sought to kill Moses. But Moses fled from the face of Pharaoh and dwelt in the land of Midian; and he sat down by a well. Now the priest of Midian had seven daughters. And they came and drew water, and they filled the troughs to water their father's flock. Then the shepherds* came and drove them away; but Moses stood up and helped them, and watered their flock... Then Moses was content to live with the man, and he gave Zipporah his daughter to Moses" (Exodus 2: 15-17, 21).*

b. **Abraham's servant met Rebecca at a well:** *"Now let it be that the young woman to whom I say, 'Please let down your pitcher that I may drink,' and she says, 'Drink, and I will also give your camels a drink'—let her be the one You have appointed for Your servant Isaac. And by this I will know that You have shown kindness to my master." And it happened, before he had finished speaking, that behold, Rebekah, who was born to Bethuel, son of Milcah, the wife of Nahor, Abraham's brother, came out with her pitcher on her shoulder. Now the young woman was very beautiful to behold, a virgin; no man had known her. And she went down to the well, filled her pitcher, and came up" (Gen. 24: 14-16).*

c. **More importantly, Jesus now sat at a well bearing the name "The Well of Jacob" as a clear reference to the story of Jacob, the father of the fathers, who met his bride Rachel at a well.** Anciently, this meeting narrative was basically the family history as the Jew used to sit with his grandchildren and tell them: "At a well, your grandfather Jacob met your grandmother Rachel" and this is the story of the well of Jacob and Rachel as recorded in the Bible:

"So Jacob went on his journey and came to the land of the people of the East. And he looked, and saw a well in the field; and behold, there were three flocks of sheep lying by it; for out of that well they watered the flocks. A large stone was on the well's mouth. Now all the flocks would be gathered there; and they would roll the stone from the well's mouth, water the sheep, and put the

stone back in its place on the well's mouth. And Jacob said to them, "My brethren, where are you from?" And they said, "We are from Haran."

Then he said to them, "Do you know Laban the son of Nahor?" And they said, "We know him." So he said to them, "Is he well?" And they said, "He is well. And look, his daughter Rachel is coming with the sheep." Then he said, "Look, it is still high day; it is not time for the cattle to be gathered together. Water the sheep, and go and feed them." But they said, "We cannot until all the flocks are gathered together, and they have rolled the stone from the well's mouth; then we water the sheep." Now while he was still speaking with them, Rachel came with her father's sheep, for she was a shepherdess." (Genesis 29: 1-9)[184].

5. Jesus, the Bridegroom, drew near to the well like Moses, Abraham's servant, and Jacob who were strangers at the places of the wells, so was He also a stranger at Samaria. And as Jacob met Rachel at the well, in the afternoon, Jesus also met the Samaritan woman in the sixth hour of the day (precisely at noon). The parallels would be clear to any Jew, as according to the previous excerpts from the Torah we can retain this equation[185]:

Strange Man + Woman + Well = Wedding

6. That is why when the (Jewish) disciples got back, they marveled as they saw Him with a woman at the well!

---

[184] The Targum gives a detailed account of what happened when Jacob saw Rachel, the daughter of Laban, his mother's brother, at the well. He says: [Jacob approached, and with one of his arms he removed the stone from the mouth of the well, and the well began to flow. And the water rose in front of him, and Laban's flock watered... and the flow of water continued for twenty years. After that, Jacob kissed Rachel and wept at his voice. (Targum Pseudo - Jonathan on Genesis). And the Samaritan woman knew that for this reason, she said to the Lord Christ: "Are you greater than our father Jacob, who gave us the well and drank from it and gave them food?" (John 4:12).

[185] Brant Pitre: Jesus the Bridegroom/The Greatest Love Story Ever Told, First Edition, 2014, P 61.

Additionally, our teacher saint John the evangelist mentioned this: *"And at this point His disciples came, and they marveled that He talked with a woman ..." (John 4:27)*. Why did they marvel? It was not their first time seeing Him speaking to a woman. As the Bible mentioned, Jesus spoke to women multiple times. For example, He spoke with the Canaanite woman (Matthew 15: 21-28), Mary and Martha (Luke 10: 38-42), and the bleeding woman (Mark 5: 24-34) but there were many women following Him as well while He was preaching the Kingdom of God with the twelve disciples (Luke 8: 1-3). That being said, it is clear that in this situation, the disciples were not marveling simply because He was speaking with a woman, but at His conversation with a strange woman at a well. As the disciples were well acquainted with the stories of Moses, Abraham's servant, and Jacob, so they thought that they were witnessing the first step of the Jewish marriage (choosing the bride)[186] which made them marvel at the scene.

7. What is even more strange for us is that it is impossible for this woman to have possibly been a bride for Jesus, even if we assume that He had intended to marry; first of all because she is a Samaritan, second of all, she has an unlawful past. And we will clarify this in detail as follows:

a. She is a Samaritan woman and he is Jewish man. And she pointed this out herself as she said: *"... How is it that You, being a Jew, ask a drink from me, a Samaritan woman?" For Jews have no dealings with Samaritans" (John 4:9)*. And to understand that, we must return to the historical origin of the Samaritans. According to the Old Testament and precisely in 722 BCE the Assyrian emperor defeated the ten Northernmost tribes of Israel, expelled them, and scattered them across the lands

---
[186] For more information on choosing a bride in the Jewish tradition, see "Choosing a Bride" In the third chapter of this book.

of the nations around them (2 Kings 17: 21-23) he installed pagan nations in their place (2 Kings 17: 24-25). The Old Testament tells us that the Samaritans worshiped the God of Israel, but they continued to worship other gods in a mixture between Judaism and Paganism (2 Kings 17: 29-40). The Samaritans considered the books of Moses as holy books and built a temple on mount Gerizim where they offered sacrifices to God as the Samaritan woman mentioned (John 4:20). And as a result of that, the Southernmost Jewish tribes did not have any positive feelings toward the Samaritans. As they looked to them as people with pagan blood, and as their rival religion with an ugly mixture of Judaism and Paganism. This is why, after the returning from the Babylon capture, the Jews refused the Samaritans' help to rebuild their temple and the walls of Jerusalem. With time, the enmity increased, and the Samaritans' food became unholy to the Jews, even saying the word "Samaritan" was considered defilement to the Jews, and the word Samaritan became a synonym for "heretic" or "dissident," that is why the Jews said to Jesus: *"... Do we not say rightly that You are a Samaritan and have a demon?" (John 8:48).* Because it was completely out of the norm for a Jewish man to start a conversation with a Samaritan woman.

b. The other reason that makes it completely impossible for Jesus to marry her, a more controversial one, is that this woman has an unlawful past. She had five husbands (John 4: 16-18). Of course, a woman may be widowed once, twice, three, or even four times, but five times is very unlikely[187]. It is obvious, then, that she was divorced more than once. And the law of Moses gave the right to the man to divorce his wife if he found her unclean, according to what is mentioned

---

[187] In rare cases, a woman becomes widowed more than four times, such as what happened with Sarah, the daughter of Raguel. He had contracted for her with seven men, and a demon named Asmodeus would kill them immediately after they entered upon her. (Tobit 3:8).

An Inspiration from the Bridegroom and the Bride

in **Deut. 24:1: "When a man takes a wife and marries her, and it happens that she finds no favor in his eyes because he has found some uncleanness in her, and he writes her a certificate of divorce, puts it in her hand, and sends her out of his house."** The Rabbis differed in defining this uncleanness (רבד תורע - ʿervâh dâbâr) some saw it as proof of adultery while others saw it as anything that may annoy the husband, however trivial, even if it was burning his food, for example[188]. Whatever the reason was for the many husbands this woman had, plurality in itself renders this woman no longer desirable for marriage. This is because the advice that was given to the man, according to the early Jewish writings is: "Do not add a marriage on another marriage, it is a disaster over a disaster"[189]. Perhaps that is why this woman had to live with a man who was not her husband (John 4:18). No wonder she lived in an unacceptable social status, one which was looked at as an immoral case of adultery and immorality.

8. The Samaritan woman is representative of all her people, as the Samaritans were also in a state of spiritual adultery[190], just like Israel. That is why Christ, the Bridegroom, came to renew their covenant and betroth them to himself after sanctifying and cleansing them.

The Samaritan God was named "Baal", the same word was mentioned in Hosea 2:16 as meaning "husband". Josephus mentions that the Samaritans had five male gods (and the Samaritan woman had five husbands), as the Samaritans also worshiped "Jehovah" along with their gods and He is not their true God as they do not worship Him alone (as the man that the Samaritan woman was

---

[188] The Sefaria Library, Mishnah, Gittin 9: 10.

[189] Richard Baukham & James R. Davila & Alexander Panayotov: Old Testament Pseudepigrapha, Pseudo-Phocylides, Wm. B. Eerdmans Publishing Co., P 205.

[190] For more details on spiritual adultery, see Sin, Jealousy and Spiritual Fornication in the first chapter of this book.

living with and he was not her husband).

9. As the bride, Zipporah went to her father, Reuel, and told him about Moses (Ex 2: 19-21), Rachel the bride went to tell her father, Laban, about Jacob (Gen 29:12), and the Samaritan woman went to all her father's family to tell them about Christ, the Bridegroom, to repent and to believe in Him and enter into a covenant with Him so that they may become a bride to Him.

10. As for the conversation between the Samaritan woman and Jesus about "true worship" and "Living Water" (John 4: 20-24). The water was used for cleansing in the Tabernacle as well as in the temple. And this water was called Living Water. The reason the man was cleansed by it was to enter the holy place of God (Num. 19: 19-20). To follow this ritual in the days of Jesus, a "washbasin" or "laver" was put outside the temple of Jerusalem for anyone who wants to enter the temple to cleanse himself and present an offering for the Lord (John 11:55).

11. Living Water is also the Mikvah which resembles the baptism and is the start of a new life. We spoke of it in the seventh step of the Jewish marriage ritual. The Jewish story of "Joseph's" marriage from "Asenath" the daughter of Poti-Pherah priest of On recounts: "And Asenath stood on her feet and the angel told her "Go with no hindrance to the other room and take off the black custom of mourning, and the sackcloth from your waist, and adjourn the ashes from over your head and wash your face and hands with the living water and wear special new clothes from linen not touched by anyone and grid up your loins with a new belt padded with your righteousness and come back to me to tell you what I should say.

So, Asenath hurried up to the next room where the jewelry box

An Inspiration from the Bridegroom and the Bride

is and opened her closet and fetched a special new linen robe no one touched and took off the black custom of mourning and the sackcloth from her waist and adjourned the ashes from her head and washed her face and hands with the living water and took a linen cover that no one touched and covered her head with"[191].

The beauty of this story lies in the way which the "Living Water" is expressed, it is the same expression used by our teacher Saint John the evangelist in his book "ὕδωρ τὸ ζῶν - to hudōr to zon". Thus, the living water was not used only to describe the water in the well or the cleansing rituals of the temple, but it also used to describe a step in the marriage rituals. Of this Rabbi Nathan says: "Wash her, paint her, cloth her and dance in front of her until she goes to her husband's house"[192].

12. If we add our certainty that Jesus Christ is the source of the Living Water to the story of the water coming from the side of the temple, we find a different prospect mentioned by John in his book. Keep in mind, dear reader, the conversation between Jesus and the Samaritan woman about Living Water as you read these next verses which were mentioned right after the death of Jesus on the cross:

"After this, Jesus, knowing that all things were now accomplished, that the Scripture might be fulfilled, said, "I thirst!" Now a vessel full of sour wine was sitting there; and they filled a sponge with sour wine, put it on hyssop, and put it to His mouth. So when Jesus had received the sour wine, He said, "It is finished!" And bowing His head, He gave up His spirit. Therefore, because it was the Preparation Day, that the bodies should not remain on the cross on the Sabbath (for that Sabbath was a high day), the

---

191 E. W. Brooks: Joseph and Asenath/Translations of Early Documents, Society for Promoting Christian Knowledge, 1918, P 46.

192 The Sefaria Library, Avot de Rabbi Nathan 41.

Jews asked Pilate that their legs might be broken, and that they might be taken away. Then the soldiers came and broke the legs of the first and of the other who was crucified with Him. But when they came to Jesus and saw that He was already dead, they did not break His legs. But one of the soldiers pierced His side with a spear, and immediately blood and water came out. And he who has seen has testified, and his testimony is true; and he knows that he is telling the truth, so that you may believe. For these things were done that the Scripture should be fulfilled, "Not one of His bones shall be broken." And again another Scripture says, "They shall look on Him whom they pierced." (John 19: 28-37)

Jesus Christ, who was thirsty at the well of Jacob and asked to drink, is the same person who thirsted on the cross and asked to drink. As He promised the Samaritan at the well to give her –along with all those who believe- Living Water, He gave from His side, on the cross, water for life. And as the water in the temple was used for cleansing, Jesus Christ, the Bridegroom, cleanses God's people –his bride- from their sin with the Living Water coming from the side of His body[193]. Then, this is the Living Water coming from Jerusalem of which Zechariah prophesied and said:

"And I will pour on the house of David and on the inhabitants of Jerusalem the Spirit of grace and supplication; then they will look on Me whom they pierced. Yes, they will mourn for Him as one mourns for his only son, and grieve for Him as one grieves for a firstborn. In that day there shall be a great mourning in Jerusalem, like the mourning at Hadad Rimmon in the plain of Megiddo. And the land shall mourn, every family by itself ... In that day a fountain shall be opened for the house of David and

---

[193] Jesus called his body the Temple, and said to the Jews: "Jesus answered and said to them, "Destroy this temple, and in three days I will raise it up." Then the Jews said, "It has taken forty-six years to build this temple, and will You raise it up in three days?" But He was speaking of the temple of His body. Therefore, when He had risen from the dead, His disciples remembered that He had said this [d]to them; and they believed the Scripture and the word which Jesus had said." (John 2:19-22)

An Inspiration from the Bridegroom and the Bride

for the inhabitants of Jerusalem, for sin and for uncleanness" (Zechariah 12: 10-13: 1).

13. The Samaritan woman was an example of the covenant between Jesus Christ and His people. Since it is a new covenant, it is not only for the Jews, but for the Jews, the Samaritans, and for all the nations. That is why the Samaritan woman was a symbol for the church. Saint Augustine describes this saying:

"It is something that is closely related to reality. As the Samaritan woman who carried the form of the church comes from strangers. As the church will come from the gentiles, a strange race other than the Jews. In this woman, then, let's hear ourselves. And confess and thank God for our sake"[194]

We are all Samaritans. Yes, we are all like this woman whom Jesus came to despise her unlawful past. How can the Holy Bridegroom come by himself and sit at the well? How can the Creator wait for the creation? Oh! How much do we resemble you, O Samaritan. How many times have we betrayed this gentle Bridegroom?! How many times have we let Him down and asked for Living Water from everyone except Him? Forgetting that he is the only One who is capable of providing it. How much have we ruined His arrangements for our marriage with our arrogance and stubbornness? How much have we rejected Him and shut the door in His face? But the strange thing is that all of this has not stopped Him, not even for a moment, from loving us. And how much has He waited for the Samaritan woman at the well? And there He is, waiting for us at the same well, even after tens of centuries have passed. He's still waiting for us to ask for Living Water from Him in prayer and encourages us to cleanse ourselves first with repentance. There is

---
[194] St. Augustin, Lecures or Tractates on the Gospel according to John/ The Nicene and Post Nicene Fathers / Series1 / Volume 7, Books for Ages/ AGES Software, Version 2.0, 1997 – Tractate 15, P 200.

no need for denial, as He knows everything (John 4:29)! But he is still waiting for us despite everything, thirsty but not for water, thirsty to see our thirst for Him!

The Sufferings and Crucifixion events

1. Crucifixion for the crucifiers was just an execution of a death sentence. The truth is that Jesus was not the first to be crucified, but before Him, with Him and after Him many were crucified on this plank that was called by the Romans the "plank of shame". Whoever considered Jesus Christ only as a prophet, will view the crucifixion as the martyrdom of a good man who fulfilled his message perfectly. While those who think of Jesus just as a great historical figure will see what happened as a strong situation for a brave man who gave his life as a price for truth and justice and died defending his principles.

But we, the Christians, do not think of the cross just as a sacrifice for the salvation of the world, but we stand in front of it, dazzled from the greatness of that dowry paid by Jesus Christ the Bridegroom, bearing the cruelty of the Romans and the shame of the Jews. Let us then explain this wonderful way in which Christ the Bridegroom decided to pay the dowry of His Bride the Church as compelled by His great love for her.

a. **Bearing the Cruelty of the Romans:**

- Josephus the Historian described the crucifixion as the most miserable of all the killing tools, whilst Paulus the famous Jurist[195] described it as the cruelest punishment. And this Paulus has written a list of the crimes that require crucifixion

---

[195] Legal Paulus: Julius Paulus Prudentisimos, known in Greek as Ἰούλιος Παῦλος. He is considered one of the most influential legalists in Roman history. He was a commander of the Roman Imperial Guard during the reign of Emperor Alexander Severus and has many valuable legal works.

An Inspiration from the Bridegroom and the Bride

under Roman law, which included treason by escaping mobilization to the enemies, revealing secrets, incitement to rebellion, murder, magic, dissoluteness, asking astrologers about the future of the ruler and a servant asking the fortune-tellers about the fate of his master[196].

- The crucified was scourged first and while the Jewish law limited the number of scourges to 39 or 40[197], Roman law knew not such mercy! Scourging was done using whips made from leather and belts with spikes or hard iron pieces or bones. And these whips were designed in such a way to make the skin of the scourged shrivel up. About this, Josephus the Historian, describes what a Roman ruler did with his captives: "They were scourged until their guts appeared, then they were kicked out, covered in blood in a scene that sows panic in his enemies, leaving their weapons and fleeing"[198].

- Murder was not the purpose of scourging, but the convict's life was spared to carry his own cross and, many times, he was scourged on his way to the location of the crucifixion. Regarding nailing the body to the cross, it was terrifying to anyone who saw it. Hanging the body was done either by stabbing it with metal skewers, nailing, or hanging the limbs with ropes. About the crucifixion method, one of the Jewish Rabbis said: "How do they hang a man? They put a plinth with a protruding piece of wood on the ground, the hands are tied and hung … If he was left overnight that would be considered a breaking of the commandment and

---

[196] Geoffery L. Phelan. M. D: Crucifixion and the death cry of Jesus Christ, Xulon Press, 2009, P 29.

[197] Sharia stipulates that the number of lashes does not exceed forty. Refer to (Deuteronomy 25:2, 3) and this was the old law. But later the number of lashes stood at thirty-nine. See (2 Corinthians 11:24). This is to ensure that the number does not exceed forty in case of an error in counting or to pretend mercy. Josephus mentioned the number of lashes in his time was forty, minus one. See Josephus, Antiq. lib. iv. ch. viii. sec. 21.

[198] William Whiston & Paul L. Maier: The new complete work of Josephus, Kregel Production, 1999, P 772.

an infringement because it is written: ***"his body shall not remain overnight on the tree, but you shall surely bury him that day, so that you do not defile the land which the Lord your God is giving you as an inheritance; for he who is hanged is accursed of God." (Deut. 21:23)***"[199].

- The cross cannot be compared with any other execution process like the cutting of the head, for example, as the convict dies quickly. On the contrary, the steps of the crucifixion were set up in such a way to make the human suffer for the longest possible time before he finally dies. That is why it was strange what Christ, the Bridegroom, did as He chose to die on the cross and rejoiced in paying the dowry this way. The Roman writer Seneca[200] says: "Can a man who prefers ending his life in pain, so he dies piece by piece rather than ending it at once be found? Can a man who wants to be hung on a cursed tree be found? To stay long, disgraced, weakened by wounds that fill his shoulders and chest? To take his breath in the midst of this long-suffering?"[201].

- The Romans used to hang the crosses in the most obvious place to the public. As the Roman writer, Quintilian[202] says: "When we crucify the guilty, we choose the most crowded roads, where the most people can watch the scene so they run

---

199 Mishnah, Sanhedrin 6:4

200 Seneca: was a Roman philosopher, novelist, statesman, and playwright, and one of the most important satirists in Latin literature. He was born in Cordoba in the province of Hispania and grew up in Rome and became an advisor to Emperor Nero. He was forced to commit suicide for complicity in a plot to assassinate Nero. Despite his innocence, Seneca cut his veins and continued to bleed quietly until he died, and the manner of his death became the subject of his most famous paintings. He wrote many tragedies and philosophical articles that deal with ethical issues.

201 Lucius Annaeus Seneca (Seneca the Younger)/Translated by Richard Mott Gummere: Moral Letters to Lucilius / Letters from a Stoic, Loeb Classical Library Edition, 1915, P 349.

202 Quintilian: This is Mark Fabius Quintilian. He was a Romanian teacher and orator from Hispania, and is considered an authority and reference for rhetoric, especially in the Middle Ages and the Renaissance.

away out of fear"[203].

What is this, my Redeemer? What made you accept that? Can the Greatest be disgraced? Can the Glorified be humiliated? Can the Highest be humbled?! Oh, how great is your love! Yes, it is Your great love which made you accept all of this suffering for me[204].

b. Bearing the Shame of the Jews:

- The Jews were crucified but not the Romans! Yes, the Romans used to crucify the convicts, who, in their view, came from lower ranks, such as the slaves and the non-Romans, but the higher ranks were convicted in other ways like by the cutting of the head. That is why the apostle Saint Peter, a Jew, was crucified while the apostle Saint Paul, a Roman,[205] had his head cut off.

- The cross was shameful, because the crucified was mocked by all those around him. And Saint Mark painted, as inspired by the Holy Spirit, the entire picture of this mockery in his book. He revealed as Jesus Christ was being mocked by the soldiers: *"And they clothed Him with purple; and they twisted a crown of thorns, put it on His head, and began to salute Him, "Hail, King of the Jews!" Then they struck Him on the head with a reed and spat on Him; and bowing the knee, they worshiped Him. And when they had mocked Him, they took the purple off Him, put His own clothes on Him, and led Him out to crucify Him" (Mark 15: 17-20).*
He also mentioned that the chief priest, the scribes and the two thieves crucified with Him also mocked Him: *"Likewise the chief priests also, mocking among themselves with the*

---

203 Declamations 274.

204 His oath to the son is annual, one of the oath prayers in the rite of the Divine Liturgy in the Coptic Orthodox Church.

205 In Verrum 2.5.169

scribes, said, "He saved others; Himself He cannot save. Let the Christ, the King of Israel, descend now from the cross, that we may see and believe." Even those who were crucified with Him reviled Him" (Mark 15: 31-32). He also clarified that the people passing by the cross mocked him: *"And those who passed by blasphemed Him, wagging their heads and saying, "Aha! You who destroy the temple and build it in three days" (Mark 15:29).* Truly, shame surrounded Jesus from every direction.

- The crucified used to be stripped naked from his clothes. That was as stripping off his last drop of dignity. And that is what they did to Jesus: *"And they stripped Him and put a scarlet robe on Him ... And when they had mocked Him, they took the robe off Him ..." (Mat. 27: 28, 31).*

- Persisting in humiliation, Jesus was crucified with two sinful thieves (Mat 27: 38-44) as though He was a thief like them, that is why Isaiah prophesied about Him saying: *"... numbered with transgressors ..." (Isaiah 53:12).* This was familiar sight at that time, as crucifixion was commonly used as a method for genocide. Josephus, who was an eyewitness to a group crucifixion incident of which many Jews were victim when the roman leader "Titus" invaded Jerusalem in 70 AD, mentioned: "When the Jewish warriors knew that they were being defeated at the hands of the Romans, they were forced to defend themselves and after the fight, they knew that it was too late to beg for mercy, as they were scourged first, then tortured with every torturing device, and before their death and crucifixion opposite to the city walls, Titus felt pity on them, but because the number of the crucified was more than 500 for every day, it was hard on him to set them free or even put them under guard. So, he ordered his soldiers to do with the captives whatever they wished, as he wanted the crucifixion site to push the surrounded to surrender. Thus, the soldiers, out of rage and hatred, pierced the prisoners and nailed them on many crosses with many different positions to set an example. There was not enough space for the crosses or enough crosses for the bodies"[206].

When they mocked Him saying: *"He saved others; Himself He cannot save ... let Him now come down from the cross ... "* Let us ask: what would have happened if Jesus (The Bridegroom) had gone down from the cross? Certainly, at that time He could have saved himself, but not the others (His Bride). That is why the church, the bride, loves the cross. She believes that her Bridegroom stayed on the cross even if He was wounded. When the time comes for the church to suffer on account of persecution, she gladly shares in her Bridegroom's his by being crucified alongside Him. As she knows for sure that nothing lifts her up but the cross and enduring pain, then she saves herself and the others as well by refusing to get down from the cross and enduring the pain to the end, just as her Bridegroom did.

"And He was lifted on the cross naked just to clothe us with His righteousness… what do You endure on Your shoulders? That shameful cross which You carried instead of me…" (From the oath prayers - an annual oath for the Son).

2. Whoever looks to the cross can see **Jesus, the Bridegroom, who is paying the dowry of His Bride**. But how can the crucified be a Bridegroom?

c. **The Crown of Thorns:**

It was mentioned in Matthew 27: 27-29, John 19: 1-5, Mark 15: 16-19 and Luke 22:11 that the Roman soldiers put the crown of thorns on Jesus as though they were saying: "You're the King? Then put

---

[206] William Whiston & Paul L. Maier: The new complete work of Josephus, Kregel Production, 1999, P 873-874.

on the king's crown".

- Any Jew in the first century AD, would know that kings were not the only ones who wear crowns, Bridegrooms in ancientIsrael used to wear them as well. The bridegroom had to wear a crown as we read in *Songs 3:11: "Go forth, O daughters of Zion, And see King Solomon with the crown With which his mother crowned him On the day of his wedding, The day of the gladness of his heart."* That is why Jesus accepted to wear the crown, to say: "I am the Bridegroom". The Jewish bridegroom used to wear a crown the day he returned to take his bride, accompanied by his friends who play the tambourine[207]. The crowns used to be worn during weddings on days of peace and joy but on war and sorrowful days, they were not worn. The Mishna mentions that wearing the crowns for the bridegrooms and playing the tambourine were forbidden during the war of Vespasian before the destruction of the temple[208].

d. The Garments of Lord Jesus:

The garments of the crucified also indicate that He is the Bridegroom. As we saw before, our teacher Saint John was the most descriptive of Jesus as a Bridegroom compared to the other gospels. That is why he was eager to mention the details of Jesus's garments and what the soldiers did with them: "Then the soldiers when they had crucified Jesus, took His garments and made four parts, to each soldier a part, and also **the tunic** (χιτών). Now **the tunic was without seam, woven from the top in one piece.** They said therefore among themselves, "Let us not tear it, but cast lots for it, whose it shall be," that the Scripture might be fulfilled which

---

[207] Philip and Hanna Goodman: The Jewish Marriage anthology, The Jewish Publication Society of America, 1971, P 71.

[208] Mishnah, Sotah 9:14.

says: *"They divided My garments among them, And for My clothing they cast lots." Therefore the soldiers did these things."* (John 19: 23-25). As for the pragmatic Romans[209], casting lots and dividing the cloth was better than tearing it or not making use of it.

- The priest used to wear unwoven clothes. And the Jewish bridegroom used to wear the priests' clothes on his wedding night[210]. The word "tunic" was used in the latter Greek text is χιτών - chitōn the same word that describes the clothes worn by the High Priest as mentioned in *"Then the high priest tore his clothes (χιτών) and said, "What further need do we have of witnesses?"* (Mark 14:63) as the high priest had to wear untorn clothes as mentioned in Exodus: *"You shall make the robe of the ephod all of blue. 32 There shall be an opening for his head in the middle of it; it shall have a woven binding all around its opening, like the opening in a coat of mail, so that it does not tear."* (Exodus 28: 31-32) and also in the book of Leviticus: *"'He who is the high priest among his brethren, on whose head the anointing oil was poured and who is consecrated to wear the garments, shall not uncover[d] his head nor tear his clothes;"* (Leviticus 21:10). Concerning that Josephus the historian says: "The garment of the high priest was not made of two pieces nor sewn from the shoulders or the sides, but it was a woven tunic with a neck opening"[211].

---

209 Pragmatism: It is called the "practical doctrine," or the "utilitarian doctrine." It is a doctrine that believes that the criterion of the sincerity of opinions and ideas is in the value of their consequences in action, that knowledge is a tool to serve the demands of life, and that the truthfulness of a case is its usefulness, and the pragmatist, in general, is everyone who aims to succeed, or to a particular benefit.

210 In the rite of Coptic marriage called the diadem, the Bridegroom wears a cape like the priest, indicating that he will be the priest of the family.

211 William Whiston & Paul L. Maier: The new complete work of Josephus, Kregel Production, 1999, P 125.

- We obviously know the closer and more clear likeness of the image of the crucified as He is dressed in priest's clothing and offers Himself as a sacrifice for God the Father, but now we can add an additional perspective for the cross and see Christ, the Bridegroom, who offers His life as a dowry for the Church His beloved Bride.

- To confirm that, Isaiah 61:10 mentions: *"I will greatly rejoice in the Lord, my soul shall be joyful in my God; For He has clothed me with the garments of salvation, He has covered me with the robe of righteousness, As a Bridegroom decks himself with ornaments ..."*. The word "decks" in Hebrew is "יְהַכ -kâhan" and literally means "becoming a priest[212]. This verse is explained in the Targum, spoken by Jerusalem who rejoices with the Lord as He dressed her with clothes of righteousness like the high priest is dressed[213].

- It is worth mentioning that the Ashkenazim Jewish men are still to this day wear white cotton clothes on the day of their wedding and on many other occasions, they call it "לְטִיק- kittel".

- As we have clarified earlier, the wedding chamber was designed to look like the tabernacle, and with that, the Jewish bridegroom who enters his room with the clothes of a priest, is like the priest in the Old Testament who enters the tabernacle.

- We must also not forget the soldiers who dressed Jesus in king's clothes to mock Him. As our teacher saint Matthew says: *"And they stripped Him and put a scarlet robe on Him." (Mathew 27:28)*, our teacher saint Mark says: *"And

---

[212] Francis Brown, S. R. Driver and Charles A. Briggs: Brown- Driver- Briggs Hebrew and English Lexicon with an appendix containing the Biblical Aramaic, Enhanced Edition, 2000, P 602.
[213] Targum Isaiah 61: 10.

they clothed Him with purple ..." (Mark 15:17), and our teacher Saint Luke says: ***"Then Herod, with his men of war, treated Him with contempt and mocked Him, arrayed Him in a gorgeous robe ..." (Luke 23:11)***. Additionally, our teacher Saint John says: ***"... and they put on Him a purple robe." (John 19:2)***. The Jewish bridegroom used to dress in expensive clothes on his wedding day. With that, the soldiers then have done Him a great service without knowing, as they have covered Jesus Christ both as a King and Bridegroom because the Midrash says: "As the King is dressed in glorious garments, the Bridegroom is dressed in glorious garments as well"[214].

c. **Blood and Water Coming Out From His Side:**

- One of the most important things that demonstrated that the crucified is a Bridegroom is the water coming out from his side. The bodies could not stay on the cross until the next day because it is against the law (Deut. 21:23). That is why a soldier volunteered and wanted to ensure that it was finished quickly. As the Passover was the day following the crucifixion day and violating the law during the feasts was very dangerous for the Romans, so they wanted to avoid it because it risked causing a riot among the people as hundreds of thousands of Jewish people come to Jerusalem to celebrate the feast and they would be angry if any violation took place.

The soldiers broke the legs of the two thieves because the crucified was forced to raise his hands and nailed feet enough to move his body up and down to be able to breathe. And the Romans were used to accelerate his death by breaking his legs under the knees by beating them with an iron hammer. This method is known as "Crurifragium", and it prevents the crucified from pushing his

---

[214] Philip and Hanna Goodman: The Jewish Marriage anthology, The Jewish Publication Society of America, 1971, P 34.

body upwards to breathe so he suffocates and dies in the span of a few minutes. However, with Jesus, the situation was different from the two thieves as the soldier stabbed Him in His side with a long spear (John 19: 28-35).

- But when a Jew hears the word "side," he immediately remembers Adam's side! There is then a parallel between the flow of blood and water from Jesus Christ's side and the rib taken from Adam's side in the Garden of Eden (Gen. 2: 21-24). The word "rib" used in Genesis is the Hebrew word 'צֵלָע - tsêlâ'' which literally means "side"[215]. If we focus on both scenes, we can see Eve, the Bride, coming out from the side of Adam, the Bridegroom, is adjacent to the Church, the Bride, coming out from the side of Jesus, the Bridegroom! Adam was naked when Eve was taken out from him, and Jesus Christ was naked when blood and water came out of Him. The first Adam was asleep when Eve was created and the second Adam (Jesus Christ) was sleeping, a sleep of death, when blood and water flowed from His side. As the creation of woman from Adam's rib was a miracle, the flowing of water and blood from the side of the Redeemer was a miracle as well, it is even a foundation for the wedding of Christ and the Church. As mentioned in Genesis: ***"Then the rib which the Lord God had taken from man He made[216] into a woman, and He brought her to the man" (Genesis 2:22).*** Furthermore, Christ builds His church with blood and water coming out from His side.

As it was said about God in the book of Genesis, that He brought Eve to Adam and she was in complete innocence and righteousness, similarly, Christ brings the Church to Himself as a glorious church without spot, wrinkle, or blemish (Ephesians 5:27).

215
216

- That is why Saint Augustine says: "In these first two humans (Adam and Eve) ... the wedding of Christ and the Church was prophesied. Since Adam was an example of Christ, creating Eve from the side of Adam while He was asleep occurred before the creation of the church from the side of the sleeping God. As He suffered, died on the cross, and was stabbed with the spear, so the sacraments which formed the church flowed from Him. Through Christ's sleep, we understand His love. **In the same way Eve came out of the side of a sleeping Adam, the church was also born from the side of the suffering Christ**".

- About the creation of Eve, Saint Augustine says: "He (God) did not take flesh from which to create the woman, but He took a bone, from which the woman was created. He (God) filled the bone's place with flesh. He (God) could have taken anything else to create the woman, flesh instead of rib. What does this clarify? The woman was created strong from the rib, while Adam was weakened with the flesh. It is an example for Christ and the Church, as from His weakness we took our strength"[217].

- Then, and as Eve was given life with a great gift which is the rib of Adam, who was considered the first bridegroom in history, so has the Church also, the Bride of Christ, been given life with a greater gift, the living water that is for the Holy Spirit in the sacrament of baptism and the blood of Christ in the sacrament of the Eucharist. As life was given to Eve and from her, it went out to all humanity, so it is that life taken from the sacraments flows from the Church to all its believers.

---

[217] St. Augustin, Lecures or Tractates on the Gospel according to John/ The Nicene and Post Nicene Fathers / Series1 / Volume 7, Books for Ages/ AGES Software, Version 2.0, 1997 – Tractate 15, P 199-200.

- Truly, you were right our great teacher the apostle Saint Paul when you described the dowry of Christ, the Bridegroom, who is the Life which gave the Church, His Bride a **great mystery**, saying: *"Husbands, love your wives, just as Christ also loved the church and gave Himself for her, that He might sanctify and cleanse her with the washing of water by the word, that He might present her to Himself a glorious church, not having spot or wrinkle or any such thing, but that she should be holy and without blemish. So husbands ought to love their own wives as their own bodies; he who loves his wife loves himself. For no one ever hated his own flesh, but nourishes and cherishes it, just as the Lord does the church. For we are members of His body, of His flesh and of His bones. "For this reason a man shall leave his father and mother and be joined to his wife, and the two shall become one flesh." This is a great mystery, but I speak concerning Christ and the church" (Ephesians 5: 25-32).*

It is worth mentioning that in the words of the apostle Saint Paul here are referencing Adam and Eve as he quoted the verse from Genesis that says: *"For this reason a man shall leave his father and mother and be joined to his wife, and the two shall become one flesh." (Genesis 2: 24)* and it was mentioned directly after the creation of Eve from Adam's rib.

The Sadducees' Questions Regarding the Resurrection

1. This incident was mentioned in Matthew 22: 23-33, Mark 12: 18-27, and in Luke 20: 27-38. Let us start with what our teacher the evangelist Saint Mark said:

"Then some Sadducees, who say there is no resurrection, came to Him; and they asked Him, saying: "Teacher, Moses wrote to

us that if a man's brother dies, and leaves his wife behind, and leaves no children, his brother should take his wife and raise up offspring for his brother. Now there were seven brothers. The first took a wife; and dying, he left no offspring. And the second took her, and he died; nor did he leave any offspring. And the third likewise. So the seven had her and left no offspring. Last of all the woman died also. Therefore, in the resurrection, when they rise, whose wife will she be? For all seven had her as wife." (Mark 12: 18-23).

2. In the first century BCE, most of the Jews believed in the immortality of spirits after death and in the resurrection of physical bodies at the end of times. It was specifically the state of the bodies after the resurrection which the Sadducees, who were the elite that formed a social class in Jerusalem, were questioning. They were known not to believe in the resurrection of physical bodies nor in the immortality of the spirit. Thus their question to Jesus Christ is considered a malicious question. According to their beliefs, the answer is already known and it is that there is no resurrection at all.

Before that, our teacher Saint Mark the Evangelist mentioned that the chief priests and the scribes tried to find fault in Jesus and when they could not find one, they wanted to capture Him, but they were afraid of the people, so they left Him. However, they sent to Him the Pharisees and the Herodians[218] to bait Him and catch any word that comes from His mouth, but they could not either. Then the Sadducees asked Him, mainly thinking that He may answer incorrectly. They wanted to mock the idea of the resurrection by

---

[218] The Herodians: Greek Ἡρῳδιανοί, also called the Hadras. They are a group that sympathized with Herod the Great, as they saw in him the expected Messiah, and they also saw in his rule what protects the nation from the oppression of pagan Rome. Herod had adopted Judaism in agreement with the Roman authorities because of the friendship and appreciation that he linked to them. And they were seeking the independence of the state. They strongly defended Herod's rule despite the opposition of the Pharisees because he was an Edomite, but they agreed with the Pharisees to hate Rome and Christ. After the death of Herod, the Great, the Herodians continued to support his family, and in the days of Christ they were loyal to Herod Antipas.

creating a strange fictional scenario of a woman who married seven times.

3. There was a law known as "marriage the sister-in-law" law or "marrying the brother's widow " as the Torah states that a man must marry his dead brother's wife if she had no sons from his brother. And if conceived from him, the children would bear the name of his dead brother and take his inheritance. The Sadducees were trying to put Jesus in trouble. Whether He rejects the Torah and the commandments, violating its laws or to deny the resurrection or perhaps to suggest an alternative solution for this parable.

4. As per usual, Jesus managed to escape this trap question and gave important teachings about God's Kingdom at the same time. Since He wanted to expose the Sadducees' ignorance of the nature of the resurrection where there is no marriage, He said*: "... Are you not therefore mistaken, because you do not know the Scriptures nor the power of God? For when they rise from the dead, they neither marry nor are given in marriage, but are like angels in heaven. But concerning the dead, that they rise, have you not read in the book of Moses, in the burning bush passage, how God spoke to him, saying, 'I am the God of Abraham, the God of Isaac, and the God of Jacob'? He is not the God of the dead, but the God of the living. You are therefore greatly mistaken" (Mark 12: 24-27).*

5. As for our teacher Saint Luke the evangelist, he mentioned more details from Jesus' answer to the Sadducees and said: *"Jesus answered and said to them, "The sons of this age marry and are given in marriage. But those who are counted worthy to attain that age, and the resurrection from the dead, neither marry nor are given in marriage; nor can they*

die anymore, for they are equal to the angels and are sons of God, being sons of the resurrection" (Luke 20: 34-36). From this previous quote, we understand that the purpose of marriage on earth is reproduction for the perpetuation of mankind. However, after the resurrection, there will no longer be death, so there is no need to multiply the offspring. So there will not be marriage after the resurrection, not because marriage is evil, since God is the one who ordered human beings to reproduce in Genesis: ***"Then God blessed them, and God said to them, "Be fruitful and multiply; fill the earth and subdue it ... " (Gen. 1:28),*** but there will not be marriage because marriage is an earthly thing, only relevant to this age which will end with everything it has.

6. The answer which Jesus provided is aligned with the Jewish tradition as the Torah says: "In the other world there is no food or water or reproduction. But the righteous ones will sit with their crowns over their heads and celebrate the Glory of the Divine Presence"[219].

The Torah also says: "Physical relations will be prohibited in the next age. As on that day the Holy One, blessed is He, revealed Himself on Mount Sinai to give the Torah to the Children of Israel, physical relations were prohibited for three days as Moses told the people: ***"... Be ready for the third day; do not come near your wives" (Exodus 19:15).*** When God revealed Himself for only one day, He prohibited sexual relations for three days, in the coming age, when His presence is continuous in the midst of Israel, would physical relations not be prohibited?"[220]

7. Jewish teachings have then connected the nonexistence of marriage after the resurrection with the incident of Mount

---

[219] Babylonian Talmud, Berakoth 17a

[220] Midrash on Psalms 146:4

Sinai. As we said earlier that the day in which the Law was given on Mount Sinai was the day "Jehovah", the Bridegroom, took "Israel" as a Bride for Him[221]. Since that day, the priest in the temple had to abstain from these kinds of relations (1 Samuel 21: 1-6), and because of that, sexual intercourse is prohibited before the Eucharist[222] not because it is evil, but because the bride who will participate in the wedding banquet (The Eucharist) should not be busy with an earthly bridegroom as her mind is busy preparing to meet her Heavenly Prince and nobody else but Him. She now does not need to express her love to her earthly bridegroom as long as she is busy thinking about how to express her love to her Heavenly One. If that happens while the soul is still here on earth, then after the resurrection when God is continuously present, there will be no room for physical relations. As this continuous presence makes the soul rejoice completely with her Bridegroom who satisfies her, so she would need nothing else. So, she would not need to marry physically anymore.

The same thing can be applied to fasting and prayer when the bride completely frees herself for her Heavenly Bridegroom, this is why the apostle Saint Paul says: ***"Do not deprive one another except with consent for a time, that you may give yourselves to fasting and prayer; and come together again so that Satan does not tempt you because of your lack of self-control" (1 Corinthians 7:5)***. Abstaining from physical relations here confirms a strong will in God to achieve discipline, it is the same as abstaining from permitted food for the sake of fasting.

8. There will not be marriage after resurrection, not just because marriage will no longer have a purpose, but because all humanity

---

[221] For more details about Jehovah the Bridegroom and Israel the Bride, see the first chapter of this book "Jehovah Makes a Covenant with Israel."

[222] His Holiness Pope Shenouda III: The Spiritual Media Series - Anba Rois Offset in Abbasiya - First / 1992 AD - p. 109.

will be a bride for God. This will be on the same plain as the day of the fulfillment of the wedding, the wedding of Christ and the Church. This is what we see in the book of Revelation: *"And I heard, as it were, the voice of a great multitude, as the sound of many waters and as the sound of mighty thunderings, saying, "Alleluia! For the Lord God Omnipotent reigns! Let us be glad and rejoice and give Him glory, for the marriage of the Lamb has come, and His wife has made herself ready." And to her it was granted to be arrayed in fine linen, clean and bright, for the fine linen is the righteous acts of the saints. Then he said to me, Write: 'Blessed are those who are called to the marriage supper of the Lamb!' And he said to me, "These are the true sayings of God." (Revelation 19: 6-9)*

And with this, the earthly unity in marriage is a symbol of the heavenly presence of God, which is considered the fulfillment of Christ and the Church's marriage. That is why when this real marriage is achieved, there will no longer be a need for its earthly symbol. And if the earthly marriage's pleasure is short time intimacy with the bridegroom, then how much more will it be with this everlasting intimacy with our Heavenly Bridegroom in the heavenly marriage? This intimacy that knows no bounds is above time.

Christian Marriage

Marriage, for many, is considered as a temporary contract with a commercial company. And according to this concept, marriage is like any other human structure, it does not necessarily have to be holy or even permanent, as its main goal is personal only happiness, whether or not both parties love each other, whatever this word "love" means to them[223].

---

223 In the Greek language there are many words that express "love". or "loving"

On the other hand, some look to marriage as a holy structure in the universe, established since the dawn of history when God said in Genesis: *"Therefore a man shall leave his father and mother and be joined to his wife, and they shall become one flesh." (Gen. 2:24).* Therefore, there should be unity between the couple for reproduction and the creation of a family. That is why the Bible said: *"Then God blessed them, and God said to them, "Be fruitful and multiply; fill the earth and subdue it; have dominion over the fish of the sea, over the birds of the air, and over every living thing that moves on the earth" (Gen. 1:28).* But when we stand in front of this great mystery, the mystery of Christ, the Bridegroom, and His Bride, the Church, as mentioned in ***Ephesians 5:32: "This is a great mystery, but I speak concerning Christ and the church."*** We find out that Christian marriage is different from every other type of marriage. As it is much greater than any contractual partnership and superior to a holy order for reproduction.

Christian marriage is a **living icon** of true love overflowing without boundaries or conditions between Christ and the Church. It is the visible image of the invisible love which Christ has for His Bride, the Church. This truth cannot be clearer than the way our teacher Saint Paul the apostle explained in his message to the Corinthians in which we see that this great mystery of Christ's love to the church cannot be fulfilled in any other type of marriage except the Christian marriage. As he says:

"Submitting to one another in the fear of God. Wives, submit to your own husbands, as to the Lord. For the husband is head of the wife, as also Christ is head of the church; and He is the

---

Including: στοργή- Storge, which indicates love through tenderness, attention and care. And there is the word ἔρως - Eros, which is a love flaming with emotions and emotions, in which sexual factors overlap and in which each party tries to possess the other. And there is the word φιλία- Philia, which describes love for friends and kin and carries the meaning of appreciation. The words ἔρως and φιλία express love only for those who deserve it, that is, for whom a person benefits from. There is also the word ἀγάπη - Agape, which is used to express absolute and unconditional love, which is the highest degree of love, like Christ's love for the Church.

An Inspiration from the Bridegroom and the Bride

Savior of the body. Therefore, just as the church is subject to Christ, so let the wives be to their own husbands in everything. Husbands, love your wives, just as Christ also loved the church and gave Himself for her, that He might sanctify and cleanse her with the washing of water by the word, that He might present her to Himself a glorious church, not having spot or wrinkle or any such thing, but that she should be holy and without blemish. So husbands ought to love their own wives as their own bodies; he who loves his wife loves himself. For no one ever hated his own flesh, but nourishes and cherishes it, just as the Lord does the church. For we are members of His body, of His flesh and of His bones. "For this reason a man shall leave his father and mother and be joined to his wife, and the two shall become one flesh." This is a great mystery, but I speak concerning Christ and the church. Nevertheless let each one of you in particular so love his own wife as himself, and let the wife see that she respects her husband" (Ephesians 5: 21-33).

Let us think ... What did the apostle Saint Paul mean when he asked the wives to submit to their husbands? Does this mean that husbands have the right to do whatever they want, and if anyone questions them, they would reply with these verses? And what did the apostle mean when he said that husbands should love their wives as Christ loved his Church? Did he write all these verses just to say, "Love each other"? Is this not an old and repetitive commandment? And what does he mean by the "great mystery"? And what does it have to do with Christ's love for the Church?

We may need to write a whole book to explain Ephesians 5 and its effect on the relationships between spouses, that is why I will try to clarify some points about what what the apostle meant in the light of the fact that Christ is the Bridegroom and the Church is His Bride:

1. When Saint Paul the apostle speaks about submission and its Greek term "ὑποτάσσω - hupotassō" (Ephesians 5: 22,24), he does not mean at all that the wife is considered lesser than her husband. As Saint Paul used this same term to refer to the Son's submission to the Father as he said: *"Now when all things are made subject to Him, then the Son Himself will also be subject (ὑποτάσσω) to Him who put all things under Him, that God may be all in all" (1 Corinthians 15:28).*

And of course, the Son's submission does not at all mean that He is lesser than Him in His nature, but they are equal. As Paul also said: *"who, being in the form of God, did not consider it robbery to be equal with God" (Philippians 2:6).*

Thus, it becomes clear that submission does not mean that the person who submits is inferior to the other one. This is the biblical perspective of the woman, she is not lesser than the man, but she is fully equal to him, as both of them were created in the image of God and His likeness as the Bible says: *"So God created man in His own image; in the image of God He created him; male and female He created them" (Gen. 1:27).* Submission then does not mean that the woman is less than the man, as submission should be mutual as Paul the apostle says earlier than this: *"submitting to one another in the fear of God" (Ephesians 5:21).*

2. Paul here does not say that the relationship between Christ and the Church is a symbol of the relationship between the husband and wife, but he said the opposite, he said that Christian marriage should be a symbol of God's great love between Christ and the Church which is a great mystery, in Greek "Μέγας μυστήριον – Megas musterion". Here, he requires the couple to look to Jesus Himself as a role model, as he said: *"This is a great mystery, but I speak concerning*

Christ and the church" (Ephesians 5:32). If this point is clear to us, it would be clear to us that Paul the apostle did not mean to put the woman in a position inferior to the man's because Christ's love to the Church does not have any desire to dominate or any cruelty which may interfere in marital relationships. On the contrary, Christ's love to the Church is a sacrificial love which is called in Greek "ἀγάπη - agapē" that does not come except by sacrificing one's life for the sake of the Bride as mentioned in ***Ephesians 5:25: "Husbands, love your wives, just as Christ also loved the church and gave Himself for her".***

That is why the apostle asks the husband to take on the role of spiritual guidance through sacrificial love and with this, he shall be a living icon for Christ the Bridegroom, and in the same way, he asks the wife to submit to the husband's sacrificial love and with this she shall be a living icon for the Church, the Bride.

3. The main purpose of Christian marriage is not to simulate Christ and the Church, but it is to work on sanctifying and redeeming the other party and so this simulation is the means for doing so. The purpose then is not just the presence of a partner in life only have offspring, but it is to pursue redemption and eternity as Christ the Bridegroom loved the Church the Bride and gave Himself for her, not just to make her accompany Him or beget spiritual offspring, but ***"that He might present her to Himself a glorious church, not having spot or wrinkle or any such thing, but that she should be holy and without blemish" (Ephesians 5:27)*** to be redeemed. And this is what a marital relationship should look like, a sanctifying relationship in pursuit of redemption.

And of this, Saint John Chrysostom[224] said directing, his speech

---
224 St. John Chrysostom: He was born in the city of Antioch around the year 347 AD. He was raised by his mother because his father, who was a commander in the army, died

to the husbands: "Tell her (your wife) that you love her more than your life. Because this present life is nothing, and because your only hope is that you pass together through this life ... tell her, our time is short and transient but if we were fulfilled before God, we will exchange this life with the kingdom to come ... then we will be one and our joy will know no bounds]"[225].

4. Among the most wonderful words that Saint John Chrysostom said about Christian marriage is what he said to the husband: "Pay attention to the high level of love. If you assume that your wife should submit to you as the Church submits to Christ, then, you should sacrifice yourself for her in the same way that Jesus did for the Church. If it reaches the extent that you should sacrifice your life for her, you should not refuse. Even if you had to endure neverending pain for her sake and do your best to endure and suffer, you should not refuse. And even if you do all of this you will not reach what Jesus did for the Church. As you are married in this situation, but Jesus did this to the one who rejected Him and did not love Him. That is why, like him, when (the bride) rejected, hated, scorned, and begrudged Him, He made her trust in Him and His extreme provision for her. Not by threatening, dominating, intimidating, or anything like that. This is how you should behave with your wife even if you saw her scorn, begrudge, or reject you, you can win her over with your great

---

early. He studied rhetoric and philosophy, then was baptized and joined the Church of God at the age of eighteen. Painted Augustus. But he retired in the outskirts of Antioch to live as a monk in severe asceticism. He was ordained a priest, then was chosen as Patriarch of Constantinople. He suffered many hardships from the Emperor and his wife, the Empress "Ephdoxia" Until he passed away peacefully in exile in 407 AD. He was called Chrysostom because his sermons were so popular that, in addition to priests and bishops, most of his listeners were slaves, craftsmen and servants. All of these people were standing around the pulpit while he was preaching his improvised sermons (that is, not previously recorded in a paper in front of him).

225 St. John Chrysostom / Homilies on Ephesians / The Commentary and Homilies of St. John Chrysostom on Galatians and Ephesians / The Nicene and Post Nicene Fathers / Series1 / Volume 13 - Books for Ages/ AGES Software - Version 2.0, 1997 - Homily 20 / P 318-319.

An Inspiration from the Bridegroom and the Bride

love for her and your compassion towards her"[226].

What a wonderful example of marital love. An example from hundreds of years ago presented by Saint John Chrysostom following the footsteps of Saint Paul the apostle and explaining the importance of the husband's perseverance to be a living icon for Christ, the Bridegroom, and clarifying that no human love, however great, may be compared to the love of Christ. But marital love still remains a continuous pursuit to reach this perfect image, the image of Christ's love to His Church the Bride.

Christ's cross is what gives Christian marriage the power to be an example of love between Him and His bride the church. As Christ, the Bridegroom, helps and strengthens the couple to carry their crosses with joy and follow Him. As though the blessing of Christian marriage is the fruit of the cross. What a wonderful cross full of blessings! Marriage then is not a cage or prison but it is a cross that both parties share to endure the pain because of love. And both have to lay their lives in the service of one another at all times, the happy and sad moments, in health and sickness, in wealth and poverty as long as they live with each other. That is why marriage is an eternal relationship, because the relationship between Christ, the Bridegroom, with the Church, his Bride, is an everlasting relationship[227] that never ceases, that is why the Bible says: *"So then, they are no longer two but one flesh. Therefore what God has joined together, let not man separate" (Matt. 19:6).*

Then, marital love reaches its highest levels on the cross. As it is tried with pain, is made known in hard times, is measured with the measure of giving and exerting oneself. As the one who cannot sacrifice does not love! Or his love is incomplete and is not perfect. But whoever is filled with God's love, his love shall increase

---
226 Ibid, P 304 -305.
227 Refer to (Matthew 5: 31, 32), (Mark 10: 11, 12), (Luke 16: 18) and (1 Corinthians 7: 10, 11).

and overflow his partner, thus his sacrifice shall increase. If he reached perfection as it concerns love, he would reach perfection in sacrifice! Then, he shall ascend on the cross and give his life willingly for those whom he loves.

5. And as we clarified earlier, in Jewish traditions, the bridal chamber was a symbol of God's meeting with His people and was designed to resemble the Holy of Holies in the Tabernacle[228]. That is why after we understand this highly developed relationship, the physical relationship between the man and woman will be holy and pure as long as it is within marriage as Paul the apostle said: **"Marriage is honorable among all, and the bed undefiled; but fornicators and adulterers God will judge" (Hebrews 13:4).** But physical relations outside marriage is a huge evil and a great sin. As the man's body is not his, but it is the Lord's who bought us with His blood and redeemed us with His death on the cross.

Virginity

Marriage was the status quo in Judaism[229]. As the Talmud says: "The Jew who does not marry is without joy, blessing or good" but it also says: "The Jew who is without a wife is not a man!" meaning that he is not a complete man, as he lacks his second half who should unite with him to become one, which is his wife. And this is also reflected in the Jewish society's perspective toward those who were not married. The Talmud says that when Rabbi "Hamnona" was presented to Rabbi "Huna" and the latter knew that the first was not married, he told him: "Do not come to meet me again

---

[228] For more information on hopscotch, see "The hopscotch and the umbrella" in Chapter Four of this book.
[229] Of course, throughout history we will find unmarried Jewish men like Elijah and John the Baptist. The matter developed through the ages from the individual case to life in groups such as the Essenes (Hebrew: םיעסא) who lived as a group in the desert northwest of the Dead Sea shore, where the Qumran scrolls were discovered. However, all this remains an exception to the rule that is marriage.

before you get married"[230].

However, in Christianity, Jesus Christ lived a life of virginity, and He –glory be unto Him- was incarnated from a virgin, Holy Virgin Mary. But virginity still seems, to some, as a strange way of life or just a way to escape the duties of marriage. Which is definitely incorrect.

1. Let us remember what the apostle saint Paul said regarding virginity and marriage:

"But I want you to be without care. He who is unmarried cares for the things of the Lord—how he may please the Lord. But he who is married cares about the things of the world—how he may please his wife. There is a difference between a wife and a virgin. The unmarried woman cares about the things of the Lord, that she may be holy both in body and in spirit. But she who is married cares about the things of the world—how she may please her husband" (1 Corinthians 7: 32-34).

Some may understand from these words that it is better not to be married, to be able to completely sanctify one's life to God without any distraction or burden of marital duties. And with that, virginity shall be the perfect solution.

But when we look to virginity in light of what we clarified about Christ the Bridegroom, it appears to us that giving up on earthly marriage has a profound eschatological[231] significance. Thus, this way of life reflects a preoccupation with eternal life. As Jesus taught, there will not be marriage after the resurrection[232] (Mark 12: 18-

---

[230] Philip and Hanna Goodman: The Jewish Marriage anthology, The Jewish Publication Society of America, 1971, P 77-79.
[231] Eschatology: Eschatology is a term that appeared during the nineteenth century, and it is composed of two Greek words: the first is ἔσχατος, which means "the last", and the second is λόγος, which means "article - talk about - lecture". It is the science or education concerned with eschatology, which examines the fate of the human soul in the end, or the fate of human beings in general.

[232] For more information on marriage in the resurrection, see " The Sadducees'

27). Thus, those who had not married and consecrated themselves to God, becoming an earthly image to a heavenly life; a life after the resurrection where the righteous live like the angels with God without marriage forever. That is why the Bible and the sayings of the holy fathers testify of the dignity to the life of virginity with its different styles. And here are some examples:

- The Lord spoke about the greatness of the virgin life in the Old Testament through the tongue of Isaiah the prophet saying: *"... To the eunuchs who keep My Sabbaths, And choose what pleases Me, And hold fast My covenant, Even to them I will give in My house And within My walls a place and a name Better than that of sons and daughters; I will give them an everlasting name That shall not be cut off" (Isaiah 56: 4,5).*

- Jesus Christ said: *"... All cannot accept this saying, but only those to whom it has been given: For there are eunuchs who were born thus from their mother's womb, and there are eunuchs who were made eunuchs by men, and there are eunuchs who have made themselves eunuchs for the kingdom of heaven's sake. He who is able to accept it, let him accept it" (Math. 19: 11-12).* And here, He clarifies the eschatological perspective on virginity, and it is to live now the same life which one would live in heaven.

- Our teacher the apostle Saint Paul spoke about virginity in detail and showed its dignity, power, and efficacy. He even wished that everyone could be a virgin and said: *"But I say this as a concession, not as a commandment. For I wish that all men were even as I myself. But each one has his own gift from God, one in this manner and another in that. But I say to the unmarried and to the widows: It is good for*

Questions About the Resurrection In the fifth chapter of this book.

them if they remain even as I am" (1 Corinthians 7: 6-8).

- Saint Cyprian, Bishop of Cartagena[233] said: "Oh virgins, look what you have started. Look at what you shall become. For there is a great and glorious reward for virtue and precious a reward for purity but, the voice of the Lord says: ***"But those who are counted worthy to attain that age, and the resurrection from the dead, neither marry nor are given in marriage" (Luke 20:35).*** You have already started taking the shape which we will become. **You truly have the glory of the resurrection in this current age"**[234].

- Saint Ambrose[235] described the sanctified virgins as the "Brides of God" for whom a glorious wedding is prepared in the resurrection, so he speaks to them saying: "a virgin is God's Bride and the prostitute is she who takes other gods for herself. What would I say regarding the resurrection through which you have received the rewards? Because in the resurrection they will not be given to marriage or marry. **What we have been promised is already with us.** The purpose of prayers is already yours. You are in this world but

---

233 Saint Cyprian: He was born in Cartagena in the year 208 AD to rich pagan Roman parents. He became a prominent orator as a young man, then became a teacher in rhetoric and eloquence. He converted to Christianity and was baptized and then distributed his wealth to the poor and needy. He grew in virtue and was ordained priest and then bishop of Cartagena. He lived a life of asceticism, prayer and contemplation, and cared for his people with purity and righteousness. He has many valuable theological and literary works. He received the wreath of martyrdom in the year 258 AD.

234 St. Cyprian of Carthage / The Ante-Nicene Fathers / Volume 5 / The Treatises of Cyprian - Books for Ages/ AGES Software - Version 2.0, 1997 -Treatise 2, On the Dress of Virgins. P 893-894.

235 St. Ambrose: He was born in 340 AD to a pious family. His father was a ruler of Gaul (France) during the reign of Constantine the Younger (son of Constantine the Great). He studied Greek, and Roman law, rhetoric, and rhetoric. He became governor of Milan. After the transfer of its bishop and when he entered the cathedral, everyone heard a clear voice saying: "Embrosius is the bishop." The voice was repeated, and everyone rushed to ask for his ordination, but he resisted and fled, but under the insistence of the people, he finally gave in. He resisted paganism and Arian teachings. He was comforting Saint Monica, the mother of Saint Augustine. He was moved by her faith and her unending tears for the repentance of her son. I was impressed" Augustine " With him for the sake of eloquence and eloquence, and St. Ambrose was able to draw him to the faith and baptized him in April of the year 387 AD. Finally, he passed away peacefully in 397 AD.

not from this world. This age has contained you, but it could not hold you"[236]. And he also wrote for his sister, Marceline, saying: "Virginity does not deserve praise because it is found in the martyrs, but because **it makes the martyrs themselves**. Who can understand, with human thinking, which nature's rules cannot contain, or who can explain in a familiar manner this which is beyond nature? **Virginity has brought from heaven what can be simulated on earth**"[237].

Because of all of this, our fathers, the monks and mothers, the nuns and consecrated ones have not wandered from virginity, but they lived the heavenly glory as a reality on earth and became brides for Christ, the Bridegroom from now on and on earth.

But the spiritual leaders, like His Holiness the Patriarch and their Graces the Bishops and ordinances, are like Jesus Christ, the loving Bridegroom for His Bride the Church. No wonder they love the Church, the bride and consecrate themselves through wakefulness and tears for Her, so they shepherd Her with the same care of the Bride to her Bridegroom regardless of the hardships and trials they may experience. Even if the Bride bothered them with Her complaints, ingratitude, and insults, they will remain, to their last breath, similar to Jesus Christ who loves His Bride and shepherds Her despite what she does.

Christ the Bridegroom in the Song of Songs

We spoke in chapter two of this book about the "Song of Songs" from a Jewish perspective. This is why it is necessary for us to speak about it from a Christian perspective.

Christianity looks to the Song of Songs as a legal document inspired

---

[236] St. Ambrose/ The Nicene and Post Nicene Fathers / Second Series / Volume 10, Books for Ages/ AGES Software, Version 2.0, 1997 – Concerning Virgins, Chapter 9, P 735, 736.
[237] Anba Youannis, Bishop of Gharbia: Memoirs on Christian Monasticism - Coptic Orthodox Theological Seminary - p. 20.

by God, as mentioned in 2 Timothy 3:16: *"**All Scripture is given by inspiration of God, and is profitable for doctrine, for reproof, for correction, for instruction in righteousness"**.*

But how can we understand the book in light of Christ being the Bridegroom?

His Holiness Pope Shenouda III, the triangle of mercy, said: "The spiritual ones read this book and increase in their love of God, but the carnally-preoccupied, need a guide in reading it in order not to misunderstand it and deviate from its pure meaning" and he also said: "The Song of Songs speaks about the eternal love between God and the human soul or between God and the Church, in the image of the love present between a bridegroom and his bride][238].

And he adds: "In order to understand the Song of Songs, we should understand it in a symbolic manner, not in a literal sense as there are verses in the book that cannot be taken literally such as (Song 6:10) *"**Who is she who looks forth as the morning, Fair as the moon, Clear as the sun, Awesome as an army with banners?**"* also the verse *"**Awesome as an army with banners?**"* was mentioned in (Song 6:4). This sentence cannot be accepted by any beloved, for how can a woman accept to be described as a dreadful and fearful lady, while women should be marked with tenderness? But if we take the sentence as a reference for the Church or the human soul, the meaning would be clear in its spiritual understanding because the Church can be dreadful to Satan and to the world"[239].

There are many strange metaphors for the Bride as her hair is *"**like a flock of goats, Going down from Mount Gilead"** (Songs 4:1)* and her teeth are *"**like a flock of shorn sheep"** (Songs 4:2)* and her neck is *"**like the tower of David, Built for an armory"** (Songs*

---

[238] Pope Shenouda III: Reflections on the Book of the Song of Songs - The Seminary of Anba Royce - First - August 2002 - p. 8.

[239] Pope Shenouda III: "The previous reference," pg. 9

4:4). Of course, these are not metaphors said by a bridegroom to his bride. When he tells her for example *"O my love, you are as beautiful ... Lovely as Jerusalem" (Songs 6:4)*, whom of us can tell his fiancée: "You are as beautiful as crowded Cairo!"

But when we understand the book symbolically and know that the Holy Bible uses a language understood by the people, we see a speech for Christ about His Church with whom He entered into a marriage covenant which identifies the commitments of each one towards the other, or about the believing soul which was engaged to Him in holy fellowship.

If He described the beauty of her eyes, her hair, her teeth, her cheeks, her lips and her mouth, all of these are metaphoric meanings that reveal her dedication to Him with all her gifts and abilities to serve him and glorify His name, which makes her look beautiful in His eyes[240].

That is why, if we read the book, we will notice a state of swinging and hesitation in the feelings of the bride (the human soul). For, sometimes, she is active and energetic while other times she is cold and lazy. While her Bridegroom (Jesus Christ) is constant, despite the state in which she is, since He always looks to her with perfect joy.

And in the book, we see the shepherd disappearing, only to come back like a king surrounded by his entourage to lead his bride to his royal palace. Just like Christ who appeared first in His human humility and who will return to take His Bride,the Church, He will come back as a King to take her to His Heavenly Kingdom.

That is why the key which solves the mysteries of the Song of Songs is the New Testament, for the Word Incarnate is the key to

---

[240] Father Abdel-Masih Theophilis Al-Nakhili: Lights on the Book of Song of Songs - St. Mark's Church in Heliopolis - Third Edition - p. 11.

An Inspiration from the Bridegroom and the Bride

the written word, as we find John the Baptist declaring it loud and clear that Jesus Christ is the Bridegroom[241].

This perspective about the book is not new, as in the third century AD, Origen the scholar looked to this book as the wedding song for the bridegroom and his bride in a symbolic charade[242].

From all of this, it becomes clear that Jesus Christ may express His love towards his Bridegroom with physical expressions, but in its purpose, it reflects spiritual love[243].

As for us, when we look at a marvelous painting, we should invest all our time in examining it as a whole and meditate on what it expresses and not bother ourselves with the chemical composition of the colors. And that is exactly what the Bridegroom wanted as He is the most wonderful artist who painted a painting that is full of references and loaded with significance.

---

241 Iris Habib Al-Masry: Reflections on the Book of Song of Songs - Al-Mahabah Library - 1981 AD - p. 10.

242 Origène: Homélies sur le Cantique des Cantiques, Introduction, traduction et notes de Dom O. Rousseau, O. S. B. (« Sources chrétiennes », 37). Paris, Éditions du Cerf, 1954 , P 392.

243 Rev. Maximus Samuel: Interpretation of the Book of Song of Solomon - Diocese of Mallawi, Ansna and Ashmounin - Church of the Blessed Virgin Mary - p. 6.

Chapter 6

The Bridegroom and the Bride in Church Rituals

These are quiet meditations to the soul that is seeking to live as a Bride, so she sees Christ the Bridegroom in everything surrounding her and especially in the liturgy[244].

The Divine Liturgy is a journey beyond time with the Bridegroom

Every person who practices the church ritual with both spirit and mind is truly living the past, the present and the future at once as though he were living above time! Living the past for the antiquity and authenticity of the ritual, living the present with all it holds in spirituality and depth and living the future for all the ritual holds from eschatological meaning, lifting the human mind to heaven and eternity where life is with the Heavenly Bridegroom. As the moon reflects the sunlight, so the church at the time of the liturgy, an earthly reflection of the heavenly kingdom.

That is why Saint Ignatius the martyr[245] says: "The Church is

---

244 Liturgy: A Greek word meaning "service", which means all kinds of social worship and prayers. This term is often used specifically for the Divine Liturgy.

245 Saint Ignatius the Martyr: He was born around the year 30 AD, and he is one of the apostolic fathers (disciples of the apostles). So The apostles saw in him his burning zeal, and ordained him bishop of Antioch. He was characterized by his zeal for the salvation of souls, so he won many nations for the Lord Christ, which angered Emperor "Trajan". He was condemned to death as food for the ferocious beasts of Rome. When some believers tried to save him from martyrdom, he said: "I am the bread of God. Let me be crushed by the fangs of beasts". Finally, the soldiers rushed him to the square, and the monsters shot him

Heaven on Earth ...". And Saint John Chrysostom says: "The church is higher than heaven and wider than the earth". And Pope Tawadros II says: "The Church is heaven's embassy here on earth. It is separate from heaven, and the only organization that can turn earth into heaven, as we say in the Lord's prayer: 'On earth as it is in heaven'"[246].

The divine liturgy truly is considered one of the most important church rituals, but it is the most important of all. As it belongs to the first apostles who were handed it from the Lord himself, when He established the sacrament of the eucharist on Covenant Thursday, in Zion's upper room in Apostle Mark's house. And the Coptic Orthodox Church prays using deep meaningful sentences coming from the heart and mind of the Bride, and organized in three liturgies[247]:

Basilian Liturgy: it is named after Saint Basil the Great, bishop of Caesarea Mazaca in Cappadocia who established it in the 4th century AD and we address God the Father in it.

Gregorian Liturgy: it is named after Saint Gregory the Theologian who was called "Speaker of the Divinities" and he was the bishop of Constantinople who established it in the 4th century AD, and we address God the Son in it.

Cyrillic Liturgy: it is named after Pope Cyril the Pillar of Faith, the 24th Patriarch of Alexandria, it was established by the Apostle Saint Mark but is named after Saint Cyril because he was the one who put its parts together and added some additions and we address God the Father in it.

---

to meet them with the face of a bash. Two lions jumped on him, leaving only a few bones left. Believers gathered his relics and sent them to his church in Antioch. The Coptic Church commemorates him on the seventh of Abib.

246 Pope Tawadros II: Coptic Orthodox Mangalia - Coptic Orthodox Patriarchate in Cairo - Monastery of the Great Martyr Marmina Press in Marriot - 1 / 2013 AD - p. 15.

247 Anba Matous: Studies and Reflections / The Three Holy Masses and the Lives of their Authors - Dar Al-Jeel for Printing - 1993 AD - pp. 10-121.

The Bridegroom and the Bride in Church Rituals

What gives beauty to the liturgy and makes it more magnificent, is praying with the church hymns, that are in wonderful harmony with the prayed texts, and deliver the words of the Bridegroom to the heart of His bride smoothly and at the same time lifts the desires of the Bride to her Heavenly Bridegroom in the sacrifice of worship.

The Church, the Bride, has truly organized everything for the soul, the Bride, to meet her Bridegroom. During the divine liturgy, the soul, the Bride, participates with all her senses to meet her Bridegroom. For here, her eyes see her Bridegroom's icons filling the church and her Bridegroom himself on the altar. Her ears listen to angelic worship symphonies presented to her Bridegroom. Her nose smells the aroma of incense, the fragrant smell of the prayers lifted to her Bridegroom. And she also tastes the body and blood of the Bridegroom in the eucharist. But regarding the touch, the Bridegroom gives her what is more than just a touch, as He gives her to abide in him: "He who eats My flesh and drinks My blood abides in Me, and I in him" (John 6:56). That is why whoever participates in the divine liturgy, it is revealed to him to be a wedding celebration!

Saint Augustine says: "Every eucharistic celebration is a wedding celebration, celebrating the wedding of the Church. The King's Son is taking a Bride for himself. The King's Son is a King Himself and the guests themselves are the Bride ... As Christ's Bride is the whole Church. From her is the beginning and the firstborn, which is the body of Christ. Because there the Bride was united with the Bridegroom ..."[248].

---

[248] St. Augustin, Lecures or Tractates on the Gospel according to John/ The Nicene and Post Nicene Fathers / Series1 Volume 7, Books for Ages/ AGES Software, Version 2.0, 1997 – Homily 2, P 934.

In Matins Prayer and Raising Vesper Incense

1. In the order of the Vesper Praises, we pray (The Psalms – The Hymn of Ni Ethnos Teero – 4th Hoos – The day's Psalie[249]) and all represent the state of worship and glory that the Bride lived in before the fall.

2. Afterward comes (The day's Theotokia[250] – Saturday's Sherat[251] or the week's Psali (Lobsh)[252] – Theotokia's conclusion) with the meanings it contains about the Virgin Mary and the sacrament of redemption. That is why it points to the promise of salvation, the bride's salvation through her Bridegroom's incarnation.

3. In raising of the incense during matins and vespers, the priest prays outside the altar, but once he finishes raising vespers incense we see him enter the altar and dresses in the white ministry clothes. This is a reminder for the bridal human soul of her old relationship with her Bridegroom[253], a reminder of the dark period lived by the Bride Israel away from her Bridegroom in a state of spiritual adultery which extended through the history of the Old Testament. But, this dark period ends with the Bridegroom's coming and His incarnation, which is why the priest dresses in white ministry clothes afterward.

---

249 Psalie: A Coptic word that means praise or hymn, and it is derived from the word 'absaltis'. any psalm. The basaliya is a rhymed piece like poetry, and often its first quarters are arranged in the Coptic alphabet.

250 Theotokia from Theotokos: A Greek word that means "The Mother of God " which was established by the Church after the Council of Ephesus in the year 431 AD, to glorify the Virgin Mary, who bore and gave birth to the Son of God the Word, and to confirm the doctrine of the Theotokos (Theotokos), which Pope Cyril I strongly defended at the Council of Ephesus against the heretic Nestorius.

251 Sherat: The plural of shereh is a Greek word meaning peace, meaning peace to the Holy Mother of God, Mary.

252 Lobsh: A Coptic word meaning explanation or interpretation.

253 Father Yohanna Salama: The Precious Pearls in Explanation of the Church's Rituals and Beliefs / Part One - St. George's Library in Shekolani, Shubra - 1999 AD - pp. 27-29.

4. In matins, the priest prays the Litany[254] of the Departed so the bride remembers her state while she was away from her Bridegroom where she becomes dead without life. Also, it is a symbol of the evil and sin spreading in the body of the Bride Israel which drove her away from "Jehovah," the source of living water that brings life. That is why the priest prays afterward (Efnoty nay nan – God have mercy on us), seeking mercy for this Bride to be encountered with her Bridegroom's mercy so she could get back to Him. While in raising vesper's incense, the priest prays the Litany for the Sick and Travelers on weekdays unlike Saturdays and Sundays and the Feasts of the Lord. As in Saturdays' matins, he prays the Litany for the Departed, and on Sundays' matins and the Lord's Feasts matins, he prays the Litany for the Sick and the Litany for the Oblations, and all these litanies are the bride's prayers for all those who need the Heavenly Bridegroom to be satiated with His overwhelming generosity and wealth.

5. Also in matins and vespers, the Bible is read, the marriage contract "Ketuba" which contains the Bridegroom's promises to His bride. His promises to love and protect her and keep her safe. Afterwards, the priest prays other litanies and they are new requests of the bride to Her generous Bridegroom who gives her according to His love for her. And because His love is infinite, His gifts are infinite as well.

In the Midnight Praise

1. The idea of the midnight praise is already built on the fact that Jesus Christ is the Bridegroom who will come to take

---

[254] Litany: The plural of Litanys is from the Greek word efsha, which means "prayer" or "seek" or "supplication", which is prayers and requests for different occasions such as the funerals of the sick, travelers, those who are sleeping, offerings, water and crops, the air of heaven and the fruits of the earth and the king or the chief.

His Bride in the middle of humanity's night when everyone is asleep! That is why His bride should prepare for His coming through wakefulness and spiritual vigil for worship.

2. The midnight praise begins with the hymn (Ten thino – Arise O sons of light) and it is an alarm for the Bride to wake up from Her sleep to worship Her Bridegroom, followed by the first Canticle (Hoos)[255] that reminds the Bride with what her Bridegroom has done, the source of victory in Her life and strengthens Her in her spiritual wars. It is like a hope for the bride, however high may the waves of evil rise around her, Her Bridegroom is capable of making a way through the deep sea and a passage for Her to walk on until She reaches the life of victory.

3. A gospel from Luke 2: 29-32[256] is read. It is the prayer of Simon the Elder, the Bride shows Her desire to be with the Bridegroom: "Lord, now You are letting your servant depart in peace, according to Your word; For my eyes have seen Your salvation Which You have prepared before the face of all peoples, a light to bring revelation to the Gentiles, And the glory of Your people Israel". Then, part of the Theotokia praising Virgin Mary is prayed as an example of the victorious Bride.

4. The second Canticle (Hoos) is recited, and in it the Bride thanks her Bridegroom for his help in her spiritual wars, for as "Jehovah" the Bridegroom once provided victory for His Bride Israel at the hands of Moses the prophet, so does Christ the Bridegroom provide victory for His Bride the Church in

---

[255] Hoos: A Coptic word meaning "praise." or " Tasbaha in Arabic ";. And in the midnight praises there are four obsessions, that is, four prayers that aim only to glorify God, and there are no requests in them.

[256] The order of the midnight praises for Sunday differs from the midnight praises for the days. Here we take care of the arrangement of the days' prayer. However, these meditations are also valid for the midnight praises on Sunday with changing their order.

her wars and lifts Her through hardships. Then the third Hoos is prayed–the Greek Psali for the Three Saintly Children, in it the Bride follows her Bridegroom with all Her heart, so the Bridegroom might come Himself and turn the fiery furnace of this world to a cool mist for Her. Christ, the Bridegroom here appears as a true Bridegroom sharing His Bride's hardships, that is why He appears with her in the furnace and does not leave Her alone.

5. Afterwards, the commemoration is recited, and in it the Bride asks her Bridegroom's loved ones to remind Him of Her state and Her needs as she waits for Him to return. Then the fourth Hoos is recited which resembles the comfort the Bride has when she is in a strong relationship with her Bridegroom. Then the days' Psali and Theotokia, where we praise Virgin Mary and call her The Holy Bride as we say in the Psali Watos on Saturday's Theotokia: "The pure bride: the quiet virgin: The Word's mother: Mary mother of the God". And we bless her as God chose her to be a home for God. For example, in Wednesday's Theotokia we say: "The eastern door is Virgin Mary the pure veil for the holy Bridegroom".

6. Then the Antiphonary[257] is read which is the biography of a Bride who lived a life of readiness, then moved to meet her Bridegroom and gained crowns, the fighting Bride reads it, so the jealousy takes over Her to be like this victorious Bride. Then the conclusion where the human soul asks from Her Bridegroom to consider Her with the other Brides who share in His glory, like the tax collector who met Him and the harlot who received His forgiveness, and the right thief who was remembered by Him and asks from Him to remember Her as well and give Her repentance to share with Him His heavenly glory.

---

257 Antiphonary is a book that explains and praises of the saint of the day.

In the Divine Liturgy

1. In Offering the Lamb

After finishing raising vesper incense, the priest is dressed in white ministry clothes that resemble Christ the Bridegroom's righteousness. As our Bridegroom is flawless, pure, holy without sin.

During the marking of the ministry clothes and the covering of the altar, the deacons sing the blessing hymn followed by Berlex[258] (Shere Maria – Hail to Mary the Queen) in which we say: "You have found grace O bride, many spoke of your honor" remembering that we should follow Virgin Mary to be a pure Bride for Her Heavenly Bridegroom[259].

There is a parallel between the bread chosen to be the lamb and all the bread put on the plate. As the Bridegroom was like us in everything except in sin (Heb. 4:15). And the Bridegroom came, was incarnated and paid the dowry in the Bride's home (earth) that is why He knows His Bride well, knows Her nature well so He is capable of supporting Her: "For in that He Himself has suffered, being tempted, He is able to aid those who are tempted" (Heb. 2:18).

After choosing the lamb's bread, the priest enters the altar, and wets his fingertips with water and wipes the bread, then puts his hand over it and prays a profound prayer, passing on his sins and his people's sins to the lamb. Here we see Christ the Bridegroom the Lamb who loved His bride in spite of the wickedness of Her

---

[258] Berlex: A word of Greek origin, and it consists of two syllables, the first meaning (around) and the second meaning (the word). So the meaning "around the word" is in the sense of a side talk on the subject or in addition to what has been said previously. In church melodies, they describe the quarter, which is said in a tone different from that of the first quarter.

[259] This melody is also said at the end of the "Sacred Sacrament of Marriage" at the end of the wreath prayer. So that the newlyweds and all the attendees at this earthly wedding remember that the real wedding is our heavenly wedding with Christ, to Him be the glory.

sins. He accepted Her with all Her flaws. And He did not stop at that, but He carried Her sins on her behalf. That is why the Bride says of Him: "My beloved is white and ruddy ..." (Songs 5:10). He is white because He is without sin and he is red also as the color of His blood. Although He is holy with no sin or evil, yet He loved the sinners, the evil, and the wicked. He loved us and died for us and washed our sins with His blood.

The priest stands like John the Baptist, baptizing the bread of the lamb with water, he declares that it is for the Bridegroom to whom belongs the Bride (the church). For this is what John the Baptist declared to the crowd at the time of Jesus' baptism: "... I am not the Christ, but 'I have been sent before Him.' He who has the bride is the Bridegroom; but the friend of the Bridegroom, who stands and hears him, rejoices greatly because of the Bridegroom's voice. Therefore, this joy of mine is fulfilled" (John 3:28,29).

After the priest finishes lifting the lamb over his head saying (Glory and Honor ...) he turns around the altar, then blesses the people with the lamb. This turning symbolizes Christ's ministry on earth which started with His declaration that He is the true Bridegroom in the wedding of Cana of Galilee and continued for around three and half years. In which the Bridegroom was roving, preparing for Himself many brides, human souls, saw His beauty and accepted His covenant and enjoyed Him as a loving Bridegroom for themselves.

2. *In the Liturgy of the Word:*

Origen the scholar says: "In the liturgy of the word[260], the soul is betrothed to Lord Jesus, and in the liturgy of the word, the soul

---

[260] In the Liturgy of the Word: includes the readings of Paul, the Catholicon, the Epixis, the Psalm, the Gospel, and the Homily. At one stage there was only the liturgy of the catechumens and it consisted of readings only, and at another time the three great liturgies were added to it: Peace, Fathers, and Meetings. In a third period, the prayer of peace was added, considering that the catechumens reconcile them to God.

enters with Him in marriage bondage]. Then this part is like the engagement phase, to get to know Christ the Bridegroom[261].

Since the church, the bride sanctifies the word of God and considers it Her marriage's contract (Ketuba) that she perseveres against the wiles of the devil. No wonder, as Her Bridegroom used this weapon in the trial on the mountain and defeated the devil, saying: "It is written ..." (Matt. 4: 1-12). That is why the Church reads from the Old Testament (The Psalms) and from the New Testament (the gospels, the book of Acts and the letters). She hears the promises of Her Bridegroom with His teachings that guide Her and light Her the way in order to live for Him alone and stay holy with no evil or sin.

In reading the letters, we remember our holy apostolic fathers' evangelism that turned the whole world upside down and brought many Brides to Christ, the Bridegroom from all the earth, brides that are not only Jewish, but from the nations as well. As we read in the Synaxarium we see a Bride who lived a life of readiness and ornamented with the crowns, so a holy zeal comes upon us to be like this Bride. We follow her footsteps and look to the end of her biography.

In the Prayer of Reconciliation, the Bride remembers Her story from the beginning, since Her creation. She also remembers the story of Her fall then Her salvation with the appearance of the Bridegroom. And in it the bride the church asks from her Bridegroom to fill Her heart with heavenly peace and to sanctify Her from every evil, deception, hypocrisy, and wickedness so that the priest and the people can continue the lamb's wedding banquet and be deserving to participate in the holy sacraments without falling in judgment.

---

[261] Hegomen Monk Zakaria the Syrian: The Divine Liturgy / A Journey to the Wedding Dinner of the Lamb - Deir Al-Syrian - 2007 AD - p. 104.

3. In the Liturgy of the Faithful:

In the liturgy of the faithful[262], Christ is present as a Bridegroom, and takes the Church, His bride and enters heaven with Her where the Divine Presence is in the midst of the heavenly ones. These are eternal moments lived by the Church with Her Bridegroom in a true partnership that cannot be described. The love between Jesus Christ and the Church by the end of the liturgy grows deeper when the Church participates in the Lamb's wedding banquet when He gives Her His body and blood so She becomes one with Him and abides in Him.

After lifting the abrosvarin that covers the altar, the priest holds the roll put over the plate with his right hand, and puts the roll that was a seal on his left hand. At this moment, the mysteries are revealed and God's presence is declared to take the Church as His Bride. This reminds us with the habit of "lifting the veil" in the Jewish marriage where the bridegroom lifts his bride's facial veil when he comes to take her to live with him. At this moment the bride glimmers with beauty as she is ornamented with the best clothes and most precious jewelry, same as the Church in the liturgy, and when the veil is lifted the Bride is able to see her Bridegroom.

When the priest says "Lift up your hearts" he tells the Church, Christ's Bride, to forget everything and lifts her heart to be with her Bridegroom only, that is why the people reply: "They are with the Lord". Here, it is the Heavenly Bridegroom speaking to His Bride, saying: "Listen, O daughter, Consider and incline your ear; Forget your own people also, and your father's house" (Psalm 45:10). So the Bride leaves everything and focuses all her thinking only with Her Bridegroom.

In the part: "meet and right", the Bridegroom takes His Bride

---

[262] The Liturgy of the Faithful: Begins with the anaphora, meaning the elevation, starting with the elevation of the epiprosfarin until the end of the service.

and shows Her His glory. When the Bride sees the glory of her Bridegroom, she cannot remain silent. So she glorifies Him admitting that He is the only Son of God, who was with His Father from the beginning, dwelling in the highest, the One who created heaven and earth and the sea and everything that is. The One who created everything that is seen and unseen, sitting on the throne of His glory, bowed to by all the holy powers. Here, the bride declares her surrender to her Bridegroom.

In this majestic journey, the Bride sees the Cherubim and Seraphim with the six wings by the spirit and listens to them worshiping without ceasing, so she shares with them in worship, saying: "Holy, holy, holy is the Lord of hosts; The whole earth is full of His glory!" and that is why Saint John Chrysostom says about this moment: "As if the man has moved to heaven itself. He stands beside the throne of glory and flies with the Seraphim and sings the holiest praise]. And Saint Cyril of Jerusalem confirms the same idea saying: "Weare speaking about the Seraphim that Isaiah saw in the spirit, surrounding God, and saying Holy, holy, holy is the Lord of Hosts. And this is why we chant these divinities that come from the Seraphim to participate in praise with the angelic hosts in what is beyond this world"[263].

In the part "Agios - Holy", the Church, the bride, acknowledges the holiness of Her Bridegroom and His love for her, this love which made Him create Her out of nothing and put her in heaven. But she violated the commandment, and lost eternal life and was expelled from heaven. But His love for Her could not keep Him away from Her forever, but He sent His prophets and in the fullness of time, our Lord and Savior Jesus Christ showed as a Bride taking the form of a man from the Holy Spirit and Virgin Mary.

---

[263] The hegomen monk Zakaria al-Syrian "previous reference" p. 121, 122.

During the sanctification, which is the next part of the liturgy that extends until the start of the litanies and is considered the foundation part, so we see Jesus Christ expressing His strong love towards His church, the Bride, as He presents Himself for Her so she remembers that "Greater love has no one than this than to lay down one's life for his friends." (John 15:13). And in His love for Her, He divides His body to give Her from it and His blood as well, so she can abide in Him and He in Her and He can become one with His bride in spiritual marriage bondage, that no man can describe. And this is what happens during communion at the end of the divine liturgy.

The priest lifts up the bread with his two hands and his ten fingers appear carrying the bread that transforms into the body of Christ the Bridegroom. In an indication that the one who gave the ten commandments and established the wedding with Israel the Bride (In the Old Testament) is the same One who is giving His body right now and establishing the wedding with the Church, His Bride (In the New Testament) held by ten fingers. The number ten is also an indication for the 10th letter and it is the letter "Iota", the first letter in the Coptic word "Eisus" that means "Jesus"[264]. And the evidence for this connection is that we pray in (Sunday's Theotokia – 1st part) and say: "… Which is called, The Holy of Holies, Wherein are the Tablets: Of the Covenant, and the Ten Commandments, which are Written, by The finger of God; They have directed us, to the Iota, The Name of Salvation, Of Jesus Christ".

We notice that there are five attributes describing the hands of the Bridegroom in the divine liturgy, His Hands are: Holy, without spot, without blemish, blessed and life-giving. These are five

---

[264] It is worth noting that the word "Jesus" It always begins with the tenth letter in most of the world's languages. In English, French and Spanish, it begins with the letter J, which is the tenth letter. Even in the Arabic language, the word begins with the letter Y, which is the tenth letter of the arrangement of Arabic letters in alphabetical order, which depends on the criterion of historical origins and not the alphabetical order that depends on the similarity of letters in terms of their writing form.

characteristics for the five fingers of the hand and each finger has its own attribute[265]. As though the hand of Christ the Bridegroom sanctifies the five senses of the Bride, as said in the psalm: "Your hands have made me and fashioned me; Give me understanding, that I may learn Your commandments" (Psalm 119:73).

In this eucharistic wedding, a huge miracle happens, as the bread and wine turn into the body and blood of Christ, the Bridegroom. This miracle is much greater than the miracle of the Wedding of Cana of Galilee. As in the Wedding of Cana of Galilee, the water turned into wine in a physical way as the taste and smell of water changed. But in the eucharist, an impossible mysterious spiritual transformation happens in the form of the physical object, in a way that cannot be understood or measured, as Saint Augustine said: "In this way, what is in the Eucharist is not just an image of God's body and blood but Christ's body itself, that He presented once on the cross"[266].

After finishing the prayer of sanctification, the priest takes the two rolls on his hands, and prays "Make us all worthy, O our Master, to partake of Your holy Body and Your precious Blood unto the purification of our souls, bodies, and spirits". And here, the church asks from Her Bridegroom, to make Her worthy to partake of His holy body and blood. Afterwards, the Bride remembers His prayers in the litanies. And says to the Bridegroom listen to the requests of the Church, the Bride "The one you bought with the precious blood of Christ" and when the Bride asks, she asks for everyone in great wisdom and open heart. So, she asks for Her peace first then for all pastors and servants, mercy for everyone, salvation for every place, the airs of the sky and fruits of the earth, the plants

---

[265] Michael Mina: Analysis and explanation of the sanctification prayers in the Divine Liturgy / with an explanation of the rich meanings of the Coptic language - Theological College of the Coptic Orthodox Branch of Bou Said / College of Pope Kyrillos Amud al-Din - p. 23-24.

[266] Hegomen Monk Zakaria Al-Syrian: "Previous Reference" - p. 130.

and the herbs and the grass and the water of the rivers. For those who take care of the offerings, the oil, the incense, the curtains, the books and the altar's vessels. And also she asks for the travelers, the sick, the dead, the uncomfortable, the widows, the orphans, the parents, the strangers, the repenting, and the confessors. She remembers categories that might be forgotten like those who do not have anyone to remember, those who want to offer but have nothing to offer, those who do not come to the mind of any, the ones in jail, exile, and captivity. And because Her heart is filled with love for Her Bridegroom, she overflows with this love for everyone with no exception. So, she prays for everyone in wonderful inclusivity, for the salvation of the world, for the married and virgins, for the enemies and loved ones, and even for those who cause heresy, so that God may dwell in their arrogance. She really cares for every man and also for all the men, so She prays for the soul, body, spirit, thoughts and intentions.

Afterward in the congregation, the bride of the Church asks for the intercession of the victorious Brides who preceded Her in meeting the Bridegroom. So she resorts to Virgin Mary as a mother for her Bridegroom and asks the saints as well to intercede for her, so she says to Her Bridegroom: "Those whom with their quests and intercession have mercy on us all together and save us for the sake of your holy name that is called over us" afterward the "fraction" prayer is prayed and in it, the Bridegroom divides his body for His Bride so the Bride mourns her sins that caused her Bridegroom to suffer saying lord have mercy three times in a sad tone.

In the end, we see a wonderful conversation between the Bridegroom present through the priest and the Bride present through the people, the Bridegroom starts the conversation by saying: "The Holies for the Saints". So, the Bride feels Her unworthiness and replies: "I am unworthy. But One is the Holy Father, One is the Holy Son, One is the Holy Spirit". And when the Bridegroom sees the reverence of His Bride and Her feeling of unworthiness regarding His incomparable holiness and life-giving sacraments, He grants her peace and rest saying: "Peace be to you all".

After that, the Bridegroom reveals that the body and blood are truly his body and blood. And the bride answers Amen (i.e. "I believe what you declare, my Bridegroom"). Here, the Bride lifts the body up high and declares Her faith that this is the life-giving body that the Bridegroom took from Our Lady Queen of us all, God's mother, the Holy Virgin Mary, and made it one with his divinity, with no mixing nor combination nor change. Then proceeds with sorrow to share in the holy sacraments and worship joyfully Hallelujah (Psalm 150). Expressing her joy to unite with Her Heavenly Bridegroom.

The divine liturgy is a taste of heavens' sweetness. Truly this wedding that we experience in the divine liturgy is like an earnest of eschatological wedding at the end of days when the Bridegroom returns to the Church to take His bride to live with Him forever.

In the Crowning Ceremony

Christianity has valued the concept of marriage. Though Jewish marriage was called Kaddushin – which means "Consecration", as it was a holy matter that yields to divine attention and although Jews looked to it as a matter that is greater than just a civilian contract, yet it never rose to the status of a mystery, as it is in Christianity which considers it a church sacrament, where the Holy Spirit dwells to unify the newlyweds, as our Lord Jesus Christ said: "So then, they are no longer two but one flesh. Therefore what God has joined together, let not man separate" (Matt. 19:6). As we clarified earlier, Christian marriage is a living icon for true love overflowing with no boundaries or conditions between Christ and the Church. And it is the visible image of Christ's invisible love for His Bride, the Church and that is what we see clearly in the rituals

The Bridegroom and the Bride in Church Rituals

in Christian marriage, that is a true image of the heavenly marriage, for the one who established these prayers and rituals wanted us to see Christ the Bridegroom in every detail of the ceremony. He wanted the wedding to be a visible image of the invisible heavenly wedding. The crowning ritual is considered a jump into heaven, and to understand that, let us remember what John the evangelist said about heaven in the book of revelation:

"Let us be glad and rejoice and give Him glory, for the marriage of the Lamb has come, and His wife has made herself ready. And to her, it was granted to be arrayed in fine linen, clean and bright, for the fine linen is the righteous acts of the saints" (Revelation 19: 7,8).

"… sitting, clothed in white robes; and they had crowns of gold on their heads" (Revelation 4:4).

"… each having a harp, and golden bowls full of incense, which are the prayers of the saints" (Revelation 5:8).

"And the Spirit and the bride say, Come! …" (Revelation 22:17).

In this scene, we see that, in heaven, a Bridegroom (Jesus), a bride (the Church), a wedding, white clothes, golden crowns, harps, incense and guests will be present. And that is what we see in the marriage ritual, the bride, the Bridegroom, the celebration, the white clothes, the crowns on the heads of the newlyweds, the deacons with the hymns, the priests lifting the incense, and the guests invited to the wedding. As if the church is reminding the bridegroom and the bride with their place in heaven, and with this heavenly marriage that awaits them given that their marriage is pure. And these are some contemplations regarding these beautiful rituals:

1. *In the Engagement Ritual:*

- The betrothed wears a ring as a sign of engagement, and the rings are golden as a sign of continuous heavenly love. The ring is worn on the right hand as a sign that each of them is a helper to the other one. Like the right arm as mentioned in "Set me as a seal upon your heart, as a seal upon your arm; For love is as strong as death" (Psalm 8:6). And this reminds us of the gifts of Christ the Bridegroom for the Church the Bride, as He gives her His Holy Spirit with his many fruits and gifts, so He becomes the best Helper for the Bride in Her life on earth as He reminds Her always of Her Bridegroom and His life-giving teachings.

- The ritual starts with chrismation, in which the equality between the betrothed is made clear. For in the first chrismation, the man's name is mentioned first, in the second chrismation the lady's name is mentioned first and in the third chrismation, the man's name is mentioned first. Changing the order of the names is an indication of equality between them[267]. And this reminds us of the first wedding, Adam and Eve's wedding in the Garden of Eden when Eve was created as a (heavenly) helper comparable to Adam as the Bible says: "It is not good that man should be alone; I will make him a helper comparable to him" (Gen. 2:18). Then, the prayer of gratitude follows where we remember the mercies of Christ, the Bridegroom to the Bride as He helped Her, protected Her, accepted Her for Himself, had compassion on Her, and brought Her to this hour.

- In the midst of the hymns and prayers the betrothed gives the jewelry to his fiancé which reminds us of the price paid by

---

[267] Bishop Benjamin: The Seminary's lectures for the subject of liturgical theology - the seven mysteries of the Church in the Coptic rite - the stages of the sacrament of marriage (betrothal - property contract - the marriage).

Christ on the cross to take the bride for Himself.

2. In the Crowning Ritual:

- In the crowning ritual, we see the Bridegroom and the Bride as representatives of Christ the Bridegroom and the Church, the Bride. In the old ritual, the Church used to receive the bridegroom first, as he enters the church in a joyful parade, and everyone is singing a hymn which was called the "bridegroom" hymn which is (Evlogimenos – Blessed is he who comes in the name of the Lord) hymn and this hymn originally is said in another celebration which is Palm Sunday, in the memorial of Christ's entrance to Jerusalem. Then afterward, they sing (Ti-galili-ah – The Galilee of the Gentiles) hymn which is sung for the celebration of Christ's entrance to the temple. Then, in receiving the bridegroom with these same hymns, the Church wants us to receive our Heavenly Bridegroom with this earthly bridegroom. Afterward, the priests and the deacons used to get back to receive the bride with the hymn "Shere Ne Maria – Hail to you O Mary" in a reference to the Virgin Mary, the pure bride of the Heavenly Bridegroom[268].

- In the old ritual, they used to say what is called: "Praise to the true bride the Theotokos", and its explanation: "Come behold this bride whom the lamb loved and wrapped up with great glory. John son of Zebedee, the son of thunder, says: "This bride shining more than the morning star. This new Jerusalem, our God's city. And the joy of all the saints is present in her"". This Bride is the church. And she is also Virgin Mary, who was a wonderful example of the Bride, that is why she was deserving of having the Son of God

---

[268] Pope Gabriel V: The Liturgical Order - Publications of the Franciscan Center for Oriental Christian Studies in Cairo - 1964 AD - p. 21.

incarnated through Her[269].

- When the sacrament of matrimony is done, in the divine liturgy, the priest takes a roll from the altar and puts it on the hands of the two newlyweds to confirm that marriage is also a holy sacrament from the church's sacraments like the eucharist. And as the sacraments are covered in an indication to the descent of the Holy Spirit to sanctify the offerings, so does the Holy Spirit's descent to sanctify the couple. And as the Holy Spirit transforms the offerings into the one body of Christ so he does to unify the couple to become one body. And the bridegroom receives his bride in front of the altar, personally from the hands of Jesus to love her as Christ loved His Church until death on the altar of love.

- The church asks the true Bridegroom many times in the crowning prayer to bless this wedding as He blessed the wedding of Cana of Galilee. Besides what we mentioned before regarding the wedding of Cana of Galilee. And on the other hand, the water in the wedding of Cana resembles the power that tries to establish the love between the couple as said in the Song of Songs: "Many waters cannot quench love, Nor can the floods drown it." (Songs 8:7). While wine resembles the strong love between them: "… your love is better than wine" (Songs 1:2) And it's said to Christ "… they ran out of wine" (John 2:3), but all they had was six jars of water (John 2:6) which means that love has disappeared in this marriage and many powers were found (six jars full of water) like selfishness, self-interest, and greed which threaten this marriage[270]. The true loving Bridegroom had to interfere and turn water (hatred) into wine (love). And it is

---

269 Ibn Kabir: The Lamp of Darkness in the Clarification of the Service / Part Two - published by the monk Reverend Samuel the Syriac - p. 239.

270 Victor Bashir: "Previous reference" - p. 8.

worth mentioning that in the past, the Church used to pray the divine liturgy after finishing the crowning prayer where the hymns chanted were the ones chanted in the wedding of Cana of Galilee celebration, and the chapter read is the one mentioning the miracle of the wedding of Cana of Galilee[271].

- The two bride-maids (two friends of the bride) carry two candles and stand on the sides of the couple in an indication of the parable of the ten virgins and to remind everyone of the importance of being ready to meet Christ, the true Bridegroom.

- The bride stands on the right hand of her Bridegroom reminding us of the psalm speaking of Christ the Bridegroom and the King: "... At Your right hand stands the queen in gold from Ophir" (Psalm 45:9).

- The priest starts praying and says: "In the name of our Lord, our God, and our Savior Jesus Christ, the Founder of the laws of perfection and the Giver of Law, we declare the marriage of the blessed Orthodox son (...) to the blessed Orthodox daughter (...)". Here, is clear that the declaration that this marriage is happening in the name of Christ the true Bridegroom and in His presence and this gives the earthly wedding great holiness.

- At the conclusion of the thanksgiving prayer, the deacons recite: "Hail to the bride-chamber adorned ... of the true Bridegroom, who has joined humanity". Thus, the church, the bride, calls all to see the true Bridegroom to their spirits which has united Himself with us to be One in Him, our Lord Jesus Christ.

---

271 278 Ibn Kabir: "Previous Reference" - pp. 230-239.

- The Bridegroom puts on a garment[272] because he will become like a priest to the family, and that is a reminder of his role and the prayers he will lead on the sacred altar of the family in the church in his house (Phil. 1:2). It is also an indication of the parable of the banquet of the King's son (Matt. 22: 2-14), in which the king found a man not wearing the wedding garments, so he ordered his servants to tie his hands and legs and throw him in the outer darkness. And Saint Jerome[273] connects these garments with the parable of the wedding of the king's son and says: "These garments spiritually represents the wedding garments given by God to the church"[274].

- Wearing the red girdle[275] is an indication for the blood of Jesus which was shed on the cross as a precious dowry for the Church, his bride. It is also a symbol that the couple are tied to Jesus. In the past, Rahab let the two spies down by a scarlet rope through the window to be a sign of a covenant for Israel's army, so that she and her family might not perish, and this scarlet rope became a symbol of the blood covenant, which makes us understand it as a symbol of the divine redemption sacrament with which we received salvation from eternal death. This is then a reference to the blood of

---

272 Garment: It is a robe made of precious cloth, all of which are decorated with crosses, which are often golden in color. It is placed on the shoulders and covers the whole body from the front and the back. But it is open from the front and has no sleeves.

273 St. Jerome: one of the greatest fathers of the West in the interpretation of the book The holy one has a great heritage in this field with ascetic and polemical articles and letters against heretics. He was born around the year 342 AD. When he was twelve years old, his father sent him to Rome, where he excelled in eloquence. He devoted himself to hermit life, studied the Bible, and learned the Hebrew language. He has ordained a priest and visited Egypt and was influenced by Saint Didymus the Blind and was also influenced by Coptic monasticism, so he recorded for us his book "The History of the Monks." About parents, he saw and met in person. He lived as an abbot of a monastery for about 35 years. And departed in Bethlehem in 420 AD.

274 Victor Bashir: What Happens in the Holy Wreath in Picture and Word - Diocese of Southern United States of America - 2002 AD - p. 45.

275 girdle in Dictionary is a belt that tightens on the middle, and the plural is gridles.

Jesus that we cannot receive salvation without. As Saint Paul the apostle says: "And according to the law almost all things are purified with blood, and without shedding of blood there is no remission." (Heb. 9:22) and Saint Peter the apostle says: "knowing that you were not redeemed with corruptible things, like silver or gold, from your aimless conduct received by tradition from your fathers, but with the precious blood of Christ, as of a lamb without blemish and without spot." (1 Peter 1: 18,19). Also, Saint Ambrose says: "The prostitute saw this, the one who lost all hope in human safety methods in the midst of the destroyed city, and because her faith got victory, she tied a scarlet rope to the window, she raised the sign of her faith in God so that the symbol of the sacred blood that will save the world would stay in memory"[276]. Truly, Rahab and her family would not have been saved if they gotten out of the house marked with the scarlet rope, as there is no salvation outside the church which is redeemed by the blood of Jesus[277]. And no marriage is outside her. And no sacraments away from this is bought by the blood of the Bridegroom. The scarlet color was a safety sign for Rahab like the sign the Israelites put on their doors and survived as well[278]. The girdle as well is a safety sign for the earthly couple as they are protected by the blood of the Heavenly Bridegroom.

- The deacons recite a beautiful hymn, the hymn of "Tay-shory", and it is a hymn for Virgin Mary. Saint Mary is a wonderful example of the heavenly Bridegroom's bride, she

---

[276] St. Ambrose / Exposition of the Christian Faith / The Principal Works Of St. Ambrose / The Nicene and Post Nicene Fathers / Series2 / Volume 10 / Book 5 - Books for Ages/ AGES Software - Version 2.0, 1997 – Chapter 10, P 604.

[277] Father Tadros Yacoub Malaty: From the Interpretations and Meditations of the Early Fathers / Book of Joshua - St. George's Church of Passporting - 1982 AD - pg. 56.

[278] Jamieson, Fausset & Brown: Commentary on The Whole Bible, Zondervan Publishing House, 1961, P 168.

truly exceeded all the other Brides. It is as if the deacons are saying with Solomon the Wise in Proverbs: "Many daughters have done well, but you excel them all" (Proverbs 31:29).

- Then the deacon reads from Ephesians 5:22 until 6:3. In it is an explanation of the unity that happens in the sacrament of matrimony which is an example of Christ's unity with the Church[279]. Then, Matthew 19: 1-6 is read where God sets clear laws for marriage and clarifies that He is the one who unifies the couple that is why no human can separate them.

- The oil that anoints the couple is an indication for the spiritual joy that they receive in the sacrament of the matrimony. And it revokes every evil work against the newlyweds and prevents the devil's warfare against their relationship. It also sanctifies the couple's minds, emotions and bodies. During that, the priest asks the heavenly Bridegroom to bless this oil to be "An anointing of holiness and purity". And that reminds us with the book of Tobias, when "Tobias" married "Sarah" whose previous seven spouses were killed on the wedding's night by an evil spirit. But the angel helped Tobias and saved him from death and asked him to burn the Cod's liver inside the bedroom.

- The priest puts the crowns on the couple's heads as an indication for Holiness and purity, as a reward for their pure behavior in life and that is what Saint John Chrysostom confirms as he sees these crowns as a symbol of victory over the desires[280]. That is why we see in the heavenly wedding many crowned like Virgin Mary (Rev. 12:1) and the 24 elders (Rev. 4:4). It is worth mentioning that the Greek word "στέφανος - stephanos" used to describe the crown

---
[279] For more information on this point, see "Christian marriage" In the fifth chapter of this book.
[280] Victor Bashir: "Previous reference" - p. 69.

is the same word used to describe the crown of thorns that Christ the Bridegroom agreed to put on because of His great sacrificial love to His bride[281].

As for us, after we have seen how the Church invoked the heavens for us in its details in the rites and prayers of the wreath, we must no longer imitate the earthly aspects of the celebration of the world, such as inappropriate clothes, vulgar songs, or other things.

In Ecclesiastical Readings

The Church, the Bride, is very interested in reading the Bible in church rituals, as she believes that every ritual sanctified by the word of God and prayer, as Saint Paul said: " for it is sanctified by the word of God and prayer" (1 Timothy 4:5). As we explained earlier, the Church considers the Bible to be her marriage contract (the ketubah) which strengthens her during the spiritual war as it is written: "For the word of God *is* living and powerful, and sharper than any two-edged sword, piercing even to the division of soul and spirit, and of joints and marrow, and is a discerner of the thoughts and intents of the heart" (Heb 4:12).

Also, the church readings that are recited during liturgies throughout the Coptic year have a profound and elaborate philosophy under the guidance of the Holy Spirit. The Church has been keen to read many biblical texts about Christ, the Bridegroom, and also about His Bride, and these are some examples from the different books of Katmares[282].

---

281 James Strong: S.T.D.,LL.D., A Concise Dictionary of the word in the Greek Testament, Abingdon Press, 1890, P 66.

282 Al-Katamars: It is the book of ecclesiastical readings (from the Bible and Synaxarium). The word is a Greek word καθημερινός (Kathimirinos) from two syllables. "kata" meaning "according to" and the word "mares" or "meres." μέρες meaning "day" (days). It is called by this name because the chapters written in it are distributed chapter by chapter on the days and Sundays throughout the year.

1. *In Katamares of days:*

- On the first day of the Coptic year (starting with Tout), the feast of the Coptic New Year (Nayrouz), and the first gospel to be read in the morning prayer of this first day of the month of Tout, we read a morning prayer from the Gospel from (Mark 2:18-22) and it contains the testimony of Christ about himself as He is the groom. There is an important verse in this Gospel "And Jesus said unto them, Can the children of the bridechamber fast, while the Bridegroom is with them? As long as they have the Bridegroom with them, they cannot fast. But the days will come, when the Bridegroom shall be taken away from them, and then shall they fast in those days" (Mark 2: 19,20). The Church wants from the beginning of the year to put Christ the Bridegroom in the eyes of each one of us in order to surrender our life to Him and become His bride throughout the days of the year.

- In 30 Touba, the Synaxarium presents a wonderful image of four brides of Christ who are the virgins "Pestes", "Helpice", and "Agape" And their mother, Sophia, who was encouraging them to be martyred, saying: " Do not lose your resolve and be deceived by the glory of this ephemeral world, so that you will miss out on eternal glory. Be patient until you are with your Bridegroom Christ, and you may enter bliss with Him." The Psalm of the Gospel is (Psalm 44:16) and it says: "Virgins shall come to the king after her, all her relatives shall come before him. They are happy and excited. They enter the king's temple." Hallelujah. As for the Bible, it is from (Matthew 25:1-13) and it talks about the ten virgins. And the Church wants to say that the Virgin is not only the one who did not marry, but she is every soul that loved Christ and lived a life of preparation as a faithful bride to Him.

- In the 29 readings of Baramhat, the psalm is (Psalm 44:13), and it talks about the Virgin, the pure bride whom God the King desired for the Bridegroom to be beautiful, so he was incarnated by her. The Psalm says: " Listen, my **daughter**, and look and incline your ear. Forget your people and all your father's house. For the king has longed for your **goodness**. Because he is your Lord. Hallelujah ". It is worth noting that the church celebrates on the 29th of every Coptic month (except for the months of Touba and Amshir) with three major feasts, namely the Annunciation, the Nativity, and the Resurrection. And if the 29th of the Coptic month comes on a Sunday, the readings of the day are read on the 29th of Baramhat, but if the 29th comes in the Coptic month on a day other than a Sunday, the readings of today are read with the prayer in the pleasant way[283].

- If we meditate on the biblical chapters that are read on saints' feasts, we will discover that they contain a model of a Bride from the Bible. A Bride whom the groom dealt with and betrothed to himself after He had prepared her to be suitable for him. However, the feasts of the Virgin, angels, apostles, martyrs, and saints, if they fall on a Sunday, the chapters of Sunday are read because it is the weekly commemoration of the Lord's Resurrection in which we focus on Christ the Bridegroom.

2. *In Katamares on Sundays:*

- The Gospel for the third Sunday of the month of Touba (John 3:22-36), in which John the Baptist declares that the Lord Christ is the true Bridegroom and that he is only the Bridegroom's friend, saying "He who has a bride, he is the Bridegroom; listen to the Bridegroom's voice: then my joy is

---
[283] Hanna Jaballah Abu Seif: Research on the twenty-ninth day of every Coptic month / Souvenir of the Annunciation, birth and resurrection - Coptic Treasures - p. 14.

complete" (John 2:29).

- Morning prayers in Paramon's Epiphany Readings (John 3:22-29). And it has the same important verse.

3. *Katamares on Great Lent:*

- Lent is the season of repentance and the renewal of covenants. It is a precious opportunity for the bride to return to her Bridegroom crying over the time she was far from Him. Therefore, Lent is considered a journey for the Bride with her Heavenly Bridegroom. Through the readings of the Sundays of Lent, the groom leads His bride to repentance, encouraging her to fast and pray. This journey of readings begins with one of the treasures (Matthew 6:19-33), where the Bridegroom urges His bride not to hoard treasures on earth and not to be concerned with worldly and bodily things such as food, drink and clothing, but rather to ask the most important thing, which is to meet her Bridegroom in His kingdom. On the second Sunday called the Sunday of temptation and victory (Matthew 4: 1-11), the Bridegroom announces to His bride that the way to victory over the machinations of Satan is the"Ketubah" which means the word of God. And on the third Sunday, Sunday of the prodigal son (Luke 15:11-32), the Bridegroom takes pity and runs with open arms and kisses the repentant, repentant bride, whatever her condition and the burial of her sin. On the fourth Sunday, the Samaritan Sunday (John 4:1-42), the Bridegroom presents a model to a real Bride, for whom the Bridegroom cared and missed, and she repented and preached to the Bridegroom, so she became worthy to drink from the fountain of living water.

As for the fifth Sunday, the Sunday of the deposed (John 5:1-18), the Bridegroom appears as a true physician to the bride's soul and body. He is the giver of healing and also the forgiveness of the sins of His bride. Then comes the sixth Sunday, which is called Baptism Sunday (John 9), in which the Bridegroom gives His bride spiritual illumination through the "Makfah" Which is holy baptism. Then comes Palm Sunday, the seventh Sunday, in which we read that the Lord Christ entered Jerusalem from the four tidings (Matthew 21:1-17), (Mark 11:1-11), (Luke 19:29-48), and (John 12:12- 19). After the eyes of the bride were enlightened and she understood her Groom's love for her, then she would be qualified for the Groom to enter her heart and dwell in it. And finally, during the Holy Week of the Pascha, where the bride shares in her Groom's sufferings with step by step, followed by the bearer of the cross, a sign of His wondrous love for her.

Prophecies on Wednesday of the first week of Joel 2:12-27, in which there is a mention of the Bridegroom, the bride, and the pilgrim (the wedding room), and in which the prophet Joel says: "Gather the people, sanctify the congregation, assemble the elders, gather the children, and those that suck the breasts: let the Bridegroom go forth of his chamber, and the bride out of her closet". (Joel 2:16). In this prophecy, he talks about the Holy Spirit and his work in setting out in the church to the great day of the Lord and preparing it to be a bride for Christ on the day of the meeting.

4. In the Coptic Synaxarium:

The whole Synaxarium, in general, presents a biography of the Bride of Christ, who faithfully struggled to meet Her Heavenly Bridegroom and deserved to receive the crowns. However, the Synaxarium is also not devoid of clear references to Christ the Bridegroom and the human soul as the Bride. Here are some examples:

- On the 23rd of Tout, which is the memorial day of Saint Takla. The Synaxarium says: "On this day is the memorial of the holy martyr Takla, the **bride** of Christ."

- Day 12 Bashans, which is the commemoration of the dedication of Saint Demiana and the appearance of a cross of light. And the Synaxarion tells of Saint Demiana that she: "When she was fifteen years old, her father wanted to marry her to someone, but she refused and informed him that she had vowed herself as a **bride** to the Lord Christ".

- On the 25th of Abib, which is the commemoration of the departure of St. Thekla. The Synaxarion says: "One of the pimps saw her and was astonished by her beauty, and he asked to marry her, but she refused, saying that I am the **bride** of Christ, so he sought her with the governor, so he arrested her and threw her to the lions."

- On the 23rd of Hatour, it is the commemoration of the dedication of the Church of St. Marina the Martyr. The Synaxarion says: " On this day is the memorial of the great martyr, the elected **bride** of Christ, Saint Marina the Fighter.

- Day 20 of Bashans, which is the memorial of the departure of Anba Ammonius the Unitarian of Antioch. The Synaxarium says about this saint: "All his hopes were directed towards a life of virginity and holiness, except that his uncle proposed to him a rich girl against his will. Since he was not able to disobey his uncle's command, he began addressing his fiancée with spiritual sayings, and through his holy biography, he was able to influence her well. He endowed her with a life of purity and implanted in her heart the tendency to dedicate oneself to being **a bride to the true Bridegroom**, Jesus Christ. The two then agreed to accept their marriage contract, determined to live together as brother and sister."

In the prayers and melodies of the church

Our Coptic Church uses, in its various liturgies, the analogy of the bride and groom, so she calls Christ the Bridegroom and the saints as Brides, and this proves the importance and authenticity of this analogy as it is rooted in the liturgy since antiquity. Here are some examples:

1. **The Lord Christ is the Bridegroom, the Virgin Mary is the Mother of the Bridegroom, and John the Baptist is the Friend of the Bridegroom:**

- "Behold, the Bridegroom is coming at midnight, blessed is the servant who, he finds watching" (The litany of the First Watch in the midnight prayer - Agbeya prayers 291).

- «Truly, you are the pure bridal chamber which belongs to Christ the Bridegroom, according to the voice of the prophets". (Hail to Mary the Queen - melody of Shere Maria Tee-oro).

- «The door to the East, is the Virgin Mary, the pure bridal chamber, for the pure Bridegroom». (The first part of The Wednesday Theotokia).

- "May He who blessed Joseph with Asenath, and Zacharias with Elizabeth, and Mary the mother of the Bridegroom, and the rest of the blessed women, bless this marriage"[284] (Blessing of the bride - Crowning prayer).

- "You are much more than a prophet: exalted in righteousness: You are the partner of the Bridegoom: the Lamb of God". (Doxology for St. of John the Baptist).

---

[284] Archpriest Youhanna Gabriel: The Ritual of Engagement and the Wreath - Principal Hanna Gabriel's Press in Bani Mazar - 1928 AD - pp. 111-112.

2. **The Virgin is a pure Bride who Deserves Honor and Glory, as She has Found Grace in the Eyes of God the Father, who Looked Up from Heaven and Found No One Like Her**[285] **so He Chose Her as a Bride for His Son:**

- "He was incarnate, of the Holy Spirit, and of Mary, the pure bride" (The eighth part of the Sunday Theotokia).

- «We magnify you with Elizabeth, with our lips and our hearts, "Remember us O Merciful One, for the sake of Your Mother the bride." (Psali Watos for St. Mary – Tout 21st and the Annual Praise).

- «The Pure Bride: The Quiet Virgin: The Mother of the Word: Mary, the Mother of God.» (Watos praise on Saturday Theotokia).

- "Today this Virgin received honor, today this bride received glory, her clothing is woven with gold, and adorned with many colors". (Today this Virgin - A tai-parthenos).

- "You found grace, O bride, many spoke of your honor for the Logos the Father came and was incarnate of you". (Hail to Mary the Queen - melody of Shere Maria Tee-oro).

3. **Wise Brides Are Brides of Christ Who Won the Kingdom, and They Symbolize Everyone Who Lives a Life of Readiness:**

- "Pray to the Lord on our behalf, O wise virgin ladies, the brides of Christ, that He may forgive us our sins". (The Commemoration of saints - the Midnight Praise).

---

285 of the Theotokos on Wednesday "The father looked up from the sky: he did not find anyone like you: he sent his only one: he came and was incarnated by you". From the midnight prayer, according to the rite of the Coptic Orthodox Church.

The Bridegroom and the Bride in Church Rituals

4. Martyrs are Brides of Christ:

- "Hail to the virgin, the true chosen lady. Hail to the true saint .... *The name of the saint shall be mentioned*... The bride of Christ". (Praxis Response on the feasts of female martyrs).

- "The wise celibate child, the chosen and true lady, the bride of Christ, saint Demiana.

- Blessed are you O damiana, the bride of the Groom, the celibate nun, the chosen and true martyr "(Doxology of St. Demiana)

- "Through the prayers of the bride of Christ, the righteous saint Barbara, O Lord, grant us the forgiveness of our sins" [286](Hymn of the intersession - Hitinites – St. Barbara).

5. The soul is also a Bride to the Heavenly Groom, so Meeting Him is a Wedding:

- "O my soul, be mindful of that awesome day, and wake up and light your lamp with the oil of joy, for you do not know when the voice will call upon you saying: "Behold, the Bridegroom is coming." So, take heed, my soul, not to fall asleep, lest you stand outside knocking like the five foolish virgins. But watch, entreating that you may meet Christ the Lord with rich oil, and He may grant you the wedding of His true and heavenly glory". (the second litany of the First Watch of the midnight prayer).

- "I have come to you O Lord, clothe me with a radiant garment and make me worthy to enter into your wedding. Let my communion with you today be forever, for through it I increase, go firm in virtue, and am strengthened in faith and in hope". (Prayer after Communion of the Sacraments).

---

286 The Deacon Service and Tunes Book: The Renaissance Association of the Central Coptic Orthodox Churches, Cairo - 1977 AD - pp. 451-452.

6. Kiahk Praises, Praise the Virgin the Bride:

The melodies are full of many statements and allusions to the Blessed Virgin Mary, the pure bride. It is difficult to list them all here, but here are some examples:

- All the heavenly multitudes, and the soldiers of the Angels, shout with melodious voices, Blessed are O virgin and Bride (Praise of Watts on Wednesday Theotokia).

- The Sun of Righteousness carried in your wombs, O virgin bride, who attained like what you have attained, Maria ti Parthenos (Praise on Monday Theotokia).

- You resembled, O Mary, the throne of God the Creator, and bore the Son of God, the alive speaking, fathers named you the Gate of the East, and how many described you, O virgin and bride. (The third interpretation on Sunday Theotokia).

- The Lord chose you, from the origin of Jesse, from a pure and pure offspring, the house of prophecy and chiefs. And you carried him in your womb, O virgin and bride, you bore him and breastfed your milk, hos Rumi Anti Leos. (The third interpretation on Sunday Theotokia).

- The chiefs testified about you, O planted vine, the virgin, and the bride, as they prophesied about you (Melody of Praise the Virgin).

Yes, you are also a bride!

Finally, and as we saw between the pages of this book, and through our review of the teachings of the book,

Holy with its covenants, Jewish traditions, and ecclesiastical rites, every Christian is in fact a Bride of Christ, the Bridegroom.

Man or woman, virgin or married, rich or poor, young or old. Yes, the way in which one becomes a bride may differ, but in the end everyone is invited to attend the wedding supper of the Lamb in eternity, where full happiness is with Christ the Bridegroom who accepts His bride when she repents and returns to Him, no matter what her past may be. He is always ready to do everything for her, even Himself.

Will you be a bride, ready for his coming?!"

www.ingramcontent.com/pod-product-compliance
Lightning Source LLC
Chambersburg PA
CBHW032254150426
43195CB00008BA/456